CROSS-CULTURAL WINDOW ON CONSUMER BEHAVIOR

Jan Callebaut
and friends

Cross-cultural Window
on Consumer Behavior

Garant

Jan Callebaut and friends
Cross-cultural Window on Consumer Behavior
Leuven – Apeldoorn
Garant
2000

197 p. – 24 cm
D/2000/5779/7
ISBN 90-5350-960-7

Editing: Jan Pollaerts
Cover design: Danni Elskens
Photos: Staf Geers

Garant Publishers
Tiensesteenweg 83, 3010 Leuven (Belgium)
Koninginnelaan 96, 7315 EB Apeldoorn (The Netherlands)
uitgeverij@garant.be

Contents

A cross-cultural window, a dialog box

A cross-cultural window on consumer behavior? A sequel to our 1997 publication, *Cross-culturally Correct Marketing*? Yes, and no.

Whereas in *Cross-culturally Correct Marketing* the authors roved the planet searching for cultural differences — and similarities — in heterogeneous countries or civilizations, the fellow travelers on this cross-cultural quest have been using a different definition of 'cross-cultural'.

The window of this collection of contributions opens on cultures that are much less apparent and obvious than those of its predecessor. Here, the 'cultures' are not geographically determined; here, the authors write about 'cultures within cultures' — which does not mean that they cannot be self-contained cultures in themselves.

In *The American Heritage Dictionary of the English Language*, we find three definitions of 'culture'.

The first definition tells us that culture is the totality of socially transmitted behavior patterns, arts, beliefs, institutions, and all other products of human work and thought; in one word: civilization. In *Cross-culturally Correct Marketing*, the contributors showed that they could find — through all the cultural differences — very similar behavioral patterns among very different civilizations. They showed that the model Censydiam applies to gain insight and understand consumer behavior is globally applicable indeed.

The second and third definitions describe culture as patterns, traits, and products considered as the expression of a particular period, class, community, or population, and furthermore as patterns, traits, and products considered with respect to a particular category, such as a field, subject, or mode of expression.

These — and especially the latter — are the cultures our collaborators are looking at through this *Cross-cultural Window on Consumer Behavior*. And they saw that here, too, the Censydiam Model was perfectly adapted to 'position' themselves in relation to the specific cultural environment of those target groups.

How could it be otherwise? Not for us, old hands at the marketing research trade, knowing all the ins and outs of the Censydiam trade. However, as you will see when reading the introductions to each of our contributors' papers, most of them are new — which does not mean unskilled or inexperienced, far from it; most are new at Censydiam.

Just like *Cross-culturally Correct Marketing*, this *Cross-cultural Window on Consumer Behavior* offers them the opportunity to introduce themselves to you and let you share their enthusiasm which all of us, old hands as well as novices, find in our work. It gives them the opportunity to play sorcerer's apprentices with the way in which Censydiam sees the world, and apply our principles to such unusual worlds as cooking, parenthood, superstition, the world of the rock musicians, and... themselves as market researchers.

To begin with, Jan Bryssinck, a psychoanalyst by profession and a marketing analyst by choice, 'analyzes' the differences and similarities between qualitative diagnostic market research such as we – at Censydiam – apply and the insight an analyst — be it a marketing analyst or a psychoanalyst — gains into the deep-seated, subconscious drives and motives of the consumer or the patient.

In conclusion, Madeleine Janssens — anyone but a newcomer, in fact one of the earliest collaborators at Censydiam — gives us a feminine, not a feministic, outlook of the next millennium. Will men, in the third millenium, only be found at 'sperm farms' as one women respondent she met in a group interview let slip in a futurological moment? Madeleine is confident that 'intelligent' women will not let it happen.

Between the profound introduction and this final knowing wink, you — women, of course, as well as men — can read all about how our new, and some not so new, collaborators see the different cultures of the world in which we live and work.

Some have been writing very purposely and pointedly, others with tongue in cheek, all — we hope — have written very readably. After all, are we not always trying to make explicit the complex mechanisms that move our 'global' civilization and trying to make them run more smoothly, for you? Are we not doing it to help you and your products fit — and at the same time stand out — with different consumers' cultures?

With this *Cross-cultural Window on Consumer Behavior,* we want to open an active dialog box through which we can actively interact.

Jan Callebaut

Jan Bryssinck *is fascinated by the "psychopathology of everyday life," by the private and subjective discourse of people. As a psychoanalyst, Jan first was confronted with it at an outpatient clinic.*

After some years, his "wishes" led him to a quite different world: that of market research. In this context, the patient is called the consumer, the respondent. Essentially, however, there is no difference: people are driven by subconscious mechanisms, and these are not always easily understood or deciphered. The psychoanalyst often sees the same neurotic conflicts show through the choice of a partner and the choice of a product.

Since 1994, Jan Bryssinck has been a researcher at Censydiam and is now Director of the Qualitative Research division of the Belgian branch. In addition to this, he still has his private psychotherapeutic practice.

Insight and self-knowledge:
an incestuous relationship

Tapping the vast riches of the unknown

One of the cornerstones of qualitative diagnostic market research such as we – at Censydiam – apply is insight. We maintain that we cannot supply the marketers with useful and practical hypotheses unless we have gained insight into the deep-down, subconscious drives and motives of the consumer. We do not put the consumer on the Freudian couch. Still, we try to open our eyes and ears for those aspects of individual and social acts that are implicitly and often subconsciously steered – just like a psychoanalyst would do in a therapy.

In this process of understanding the consumer, a number of aspects are quite important.

First, there is the fact that we try to understand the consumer *emotionally*. Secondly, there is the *position of the researchers themselves*: they are being confronted with numerous private histories that they must place within a frame of reference. Thereby, however, they have to deal with their own blind spots, inconsistencies, and subjectivity. Both points are not only of crucial importance in market research but also play a central role in psychoanalytical therapy.

The patient's insight into his situation obtained by psychoanalytical therapy, is the product of a process of change and not the cause – the starting point. The moment a patient emotionally understands a condition must be seen as the result of an anterior change – a change that in its turn is the product of an insight. Emotional insight is the outcome of a change that takes place in a deeper, subconscious, level.

With his interpretations, the therapist helps the patient to get insight. Finding out the private – subjective – truth is a game of listening, interpreting and giving feedback. In this, the timing – the moment at which one gives the interpretation – is extremely important: it heightens the chance of success – i.e. the patients' emotional recognition. Transference and countertransference are two factors of interaction that are an essential part in influencing interpretation. Therefore, gaining control of those mechanisms – by being conscious of them and putting them in their right place within the discourse of the patient – is an essential part of a successful therapy.

Going back to the relation between psychoanalytic practice and diagnostic market research, we must say that the market researcher cannot be identified with the silent psychoanalyst – who listens and registers – but with someone who, from the same analytic angle of equal attention, actively questions the consumer, *and* himself, too, in order to be able to propose a subjective truth that is troubled as little as possible by self-knowledge.

Psychoanalysis:
not the truth but the servant of the truth

In psychoanalysis, the point is that the analyst tries to understand the world in which the patient finds himself. Why is patient X afraid of spiders? Why does patient Y battle against feelings of inferiority? The moment this is understood – in the sense of being sensed rather than rationalized – is the moment the analyst as well as the patient understand this behavior emotionally and gain insight into it.

I often have experienced that insight or understanding that does not rest on an emotional apperception by the patient is throwing seed on the rocks. Only a conjunct discovery of subconscious behavior – shared by the patient and the analyst – can bring the patient to the experience of a subjective truth.

The key question however is how to arrive at this emotional comprehension, this insight, this subjective truth.

Before giving the answer to this question, it is important to bear in mind that a psychoanalyst does not pretend to have a monopoly on truth but rather tries to restore the possibility of discovering the truth. Psychoanalysis is the servant of truth and does not pretend to know it all.

On this point, the relation with qualitative diagnostic market research is evident. The researcher is not the one who, on his own authority and self-knowledge, offers the company a bestseller; he is the one who presents, on the basis of the valorization of private declarations by numerous respondents, a shared truth – a truth shared by the consumer and the researcher.

Serving the truth or "restoring the way to discovering the truth" is a question of understanding how changes in an individual are coming about. During the preliminary conversations – the intake conversations – before the beginning of the actual therapy, patients have repeatedly asked me what a psychoanalytically oriented therapy in fact implied and how it could "cure" unpleasant symptoms.

I must admit that, initially, I may have sent patients home in total confusion and with false hopes. In short, my answer amounted to this: I told them that free association was an important technique that would allow me to come to a point where I could make an interpretation and inform them of it. At that time, I called it "making an interpretation" and silently assumed that this would operate a change in the patient. That was how it is described in textbooks and that – I thought – was the way I heard it from the mouths of eminent speakers at congresses. When progress failed to appear or patients even broke off the therapy, I thought that I myself and my inadequate approach were to blame.

Paradoxical as it may seem, what I had overlooked was the fact that people are not guided by rationality alone and that the – interpretative – words of the psychoanalyst can only partially provide hope of change.

A familiar situation is that in which people talking with someone of whom they learn that he or she is a psychologist suddenly feel inhibited. They will react with "I'd better watch my words or what will you think of me – next you'll psyche me out." I used to be blinded by the thought that there could be an element of truth in this "popular belief" and that I could confine myself to enact that visionary role and make my patients face the facts by holding up a mirror to their behavior.

Being "wise" to people, or patients, is a necessary but not sufficient to bring about change in the individual, or the patient; it is but half the work. As long as the patient himself does not give a sign of recognition of the proposed interpretation, change or insight – in the classical psychoanalytical sense of the word – is out of the question.

Change does not occur as a consequence of the act – the intervention or the interpretation – of the analyst. The French psychoanalyst Jacques Lacan has called this phenomenon the master discourse – i.e. a discourse that takes its departure from the assumption that only the analyst knows what is good for the patient. In numberless papers and throughout his lifework, Lacan has tried to make clear that, in a therapeutic context, this is doomed to fail.

Besides, this belief seems to stem from René Descartes' famous assertion: Cogito, ergo sum [I think, therefore I am] in which lies the idea that thinking is an exclusive activity of the Ego, which should be separated from what happens in the external world. Of course, this is not true and every qualified psychoanalyst knows it. In P.C. Kuyper's textbook *Hoofdsom der psychiatrie* [Sum Total of Psychiatry] (1980), it says: "Insight is an insight in which one is personally involved; it is an existential insight. A merely rational insight into inner problems can be the consequence of psychotherapy that failed."

A frequently occurring phenomenon in a therapeutic treatment is the point where the patient T. repeatedly maintains that he sees what is happening to him – such as being besieged by somber and negative thoughts without being able to point to an apparent reason – but does not know how to change it. A subconscious mechanism brings the patient again and again into this depressive situation and he cannot master it. A sort of subconscious stubbornness – a mechanism over which the patient cannot control – makes the complaint repeat itself. Bystanders who mean well towards the patient sometimes reproach him, or her, with being obstinate and self-willed since he, or she, continues displaying the same behavior. The patient continues complaining about feelings of depression. His acquaintances tell him, or her, to leave of complaining and go out look for a job, get a life, seek a companion, and so forth. Yet, the patient does not succeed in turning the situation around and withdraws even more.

Initially, the difficult progress in the therapy with the aforementioned patient T. was the consequence of the installation of a transference and countertransference relation. His plaintive behavior, which he amply displayed in therapy, too, had evoked with me feelings and frustrations that I did not bring up during the sessions. Instead, I continued making interpretations that had the intention to explicate what happened with him. The effect was that he became rationally convinced that he had to take responsibility for his own life; however, there it stopped.

If logic is the sun, intuition is the moon

My interpretations made patient T. see the sun but he did not feel its warmth. In his dictionary of psychology, Carl G. Jung says the following about that: "Psychic adaptation will be grounded entirely on intuition." Does that mean that patient T. forgot as it were to follow his intuition? No. What had happened was that he had become disconnected from his own, emotional, intuitive insight into how he could get out of the situation himself. Therefore he repeated again and again what he already knew – namely a life characterized by periods of depressive feelings and powerlessness.

We follow Jung when he puts that intuition is a subconscious creative process in which images, impressions, experiences, and feelings get the value of insight. Intuitive insight must always be conformed by an experience before the patient will actually observe change.

From the moment I discussed the transference, notably the feelings the patients stirred up in me, the patient reported that he began feeling better little by little. Instead of confronting him over and again with his behavior, we cleared a space for a discourse that gave him the chance to put into words what he felt in his relations with people. His feelings of inferiority, his lowly self-assurance, and his defeatism were the consequences of an education by a domineering and authoritarian father who had always given him the feeling that he was worthless, a failure, a loser. The more the patient tried to do his best, the more he failed. Now he felt failing in his adult life, too, because he did not have a decent job, because he could not maintain relations, and was convinced of the fact that he had nothing to offer.

During the sessions, he did no longer recount what he did but what he felt and how my interventions brought him again into contact with recollections that apparently seemed to be banal details but now acquired the value of an important indicator, an emotional recognition. Later still, in the course of our conversations, he told me more often about positive experiences and contacts through which he discovered that he had been led by his feelings rather than by his – rational – convictions.

The subjective self-willed knowledge that had kept him captive in an unbearable repetitiveness had changed into a self-knowledge, a personal, emotional, intuitive insight that gave his life once more a positive form.

Maximizing the capacity to arrive at subjective truth

In itself, the way in which we interview consumers in a qualitative market study in accordance with the Censydiam model is not different from the therapeutic situation as described above. By applying projective and allegoric techniques, we try to get a representation of the motives that steer consumers in relation with a product, brand, and/or service.

Although the transference situation in itself, in contrast with a therapeutic context, is not discussed during an individual interview with a respondent, we take the view that the feelings aroused in the researchers through their contact with the respondents are crucial in the emotional and subjective understanding of the consumer.

These impressions and feelings form the basis as well as the touchstone of our hypotheses. Not only by giving the details of the consumers' stories a place within the context of the aim of our research but also by putting ourselves into question – as human beings and as researchers – we can arrive at clear insights.

This fruitful cross-pollination between private histories – i.e. the respondents' subjective truth – and the insights, impressions and self-knowledge of the researcher is the breeding-ground for a valuable and founded analysis. Just like in psychotherapy, "success" or "failure" of a study also depends on the extent in which the researchers are aware of their blind spots or their self-willed knowledge.

A good researcher listens to the respondents with an open and unprejudiced mind, arranges and conforms this information to their own insights and expertise. It is also important to continue asking oneself which impressions and feelings respondents have aroused in the researcher – just like the analyst uses the feelings the patients arouse in himself as a compass.

Keeping out and not allowing one's own emotions and intuitive feelings to play a role would be as erroneous as counting on one's own knowledge and treating the respondents' histories as a validation of one's own judgement. Personal knowledge should be implemented into the analysis so as to elevate the respondents' impressions to a metalevel.

Just like the analyst accepts his patient's paradoxical behavior – and does not interpret it as being pathological – the researcher – and the marketer – should also accept that consumer behavior is often steered by illogical and paradoxical mechanisms. To help researchers deal with those paradoxes, Censydiam has developed a software package called The Illogic Algorithm. A comparison between this Illogic program for the researcher and a teaching analysis for the formation of a psychoanalyst does hold true in the sense that both allow making mechanisms visible and thus discussible, too –

just like the responses from the teaching psychoanalyst open the eyes of the future analyst.

The fact that as a researcher one is conscious of certain – for example compensatory – mechanisms permits to arrive at affirmations and marketing recommendation that are better founded.

Frédéric Clérin *graduated in Social and Industrial Psychology at the Catholic University of Louvain. Then he pursued a course of study in Human Resources Management.*

When he began to work for Censydiam Brussels in 1996, he discovered Qualitative Marketing, which became his new passion. He has been researching mainly in the field of cigarettes and automobiles.

Some people go for a spin in their car to relax. Others puff on a cigarette. Frédéric does not smoke. And he drives his car only to go to work. In the weekend, he rolls his sleeves up and relaxes with... hard work: restoring a two-centuries-old house in the country. In his leisure time, Frédéric is a pragmatic romanticist.

His latest work on a Human Resources project approached in marketing terms meant a return to his first love without however leaving his marketing spouse. This sort of intellectual polygamy prompted him to write this contribution on man – and woman – in the peculiar cultural context of the enterprise.

Understanding man in a specific culture: a company

In this paper, I will try to understand companies in a qualitative marketing approach. Indeed, the work environment and the companies are specific worlds. They become impregnated by cultures but they also impregnate the 'locals,' the human beings, wherever they come from. From that point of view, this working environment can be considered as a culture. Don't we speak about 'corporate culture'?

How can marketing help us with respect to work and the functioning of companies?

Just like for the consumption of goods, work is a motivated action. It requires attention; it is based on wishes and expectations, and finally it provides satisfaction or dissatisfaction. Work is motivated by various things depending on humans: fears, anxiety, wishes, and expectations. Therefore, we can talk about 'motivational approach' for workers just the same as we do for consumers.

I will try to determine in which way work and companies are a specific culture, i.e. that they have specific dimensions compared to local consumption cultures. I will try to understand the different elements that belong to the motivation of working, of participating in and staying with the company, in other words: consuming it.

These notes have no historical or philosophical ambitions. Nevertheless, we can say that, at the end of the 20th century, a job is an exchange between a competence and an income. Men have specialized and do not really produce goods themselves but do participate in a production process in a rather diffuse way. Working in a company becomes a necessity that will concern the whole population even if there are differences in the attitude towards work.

What does working for a company mean?

"The company will commercialize my competence, my products."
"I will participate in the manufacturing of a product or provide a service that the company offers."
"The company will provide me with tools and I will use them to create something."
"The company will pay me instead of the clients."

First, we can observe that the ways to formulate and explain work are very different. In fact, they follow the expectations one has with respect to work but also the relationship with the company and one's own involvement. We can define working for a company in many different ways because the perception is emotionally and affectively colored. Working for a company could be considered similarly to choosing a TV program, working out vacation plans, choosing a car and so forth. Working for a company is consuming the company because it is not a unilateral act – it is an exchange.

The choice of a product, a brand, or a concept depends on the possibility to recognize oneself in it. It is in fact the potentiality to find satisfaction and to acquire its character. We can indeed transpose this to a company. Still, there is one exception: since work is a necessity, the dissatisfaction of the consumer will not lead to a direct break or to disloyalty: one can continue working for a company even if the work creates dissatisfaction.

"I've tried this soup but I was dissatisfied and that's why I've never again bought it."

This sentence is an illustration of the relationship with a quite simple consumable. It will not create a long-term relationship unless one has stocked up on it.

"I've quite a few problems with this car but I've bought it only recently and it's such a beauty and it goes so fast."

This declaration can also be related to 'company consuming' inasmuch as it is a long-term relationship and because the product has different attributes, some of which can be satisfactory and others not.

Hence, I will try to see how a company can be a consumable, what kind of consumable it is, and how the company environment – the specific culture of the company – can interfere with the relation between the worker and the company – i.e. the 'consumer' and the company.

If we consider that, in a certain sense, working is consuming, in what way is the world of work, the world of the company for which one works, different then from the world of leisure, from the world 'outside work'?

First of all, a company is multidimensional

A company is, in a certain sense, a multidimensional product of which I will present a structured and summarizing account.

A company is first of all *a name or a brand*. It can be differently interpreted, but when the worker insists on this fact, the name of the company is indeed differentiating and carries sa certain prestige.

"I'm working at..."

The *functioning of work* is influenced by the hierarchy, the rules, the responsibilities, the autonomy one is offered; the way in which authority is gained and exercised, and the division of tasks determine the framework of the labor.

This dimension does not concern the content of work but indicates how one will work. Hence, the functioning of work will be seen in different ways, depending on the 'consumers' present but also depending on the departments or persons in charge in larger companies. This functioning is often as official as unofficial. Methods of working take form spontaneously or as a reaction against a system that does not work efficiently.

"It is extremely difficult to work with such procedures."
"Sometimes I am asked to take responsibilities that terrify me."

The *content* of work refers to the trade name of the company: its goals, its finality. In this context, one appeals to the competencies or the knowledge of the workers: this is what they produce or it is their contribution to the company. The content of the work of certain employees does not necessarily refer to the finality of the company. Think of all the departments that support the production but at the same time dissociate the workers from the company brand.

"I have been working in this sector for fifteen years now and I don't know a thing about it."
"What excites me is resolving technical problems but for the rest..."

Companies are also composed of *people*, of individuals who by themselves can put their marks on the company. Therefore, a personality, a key position, will determine the culture, the ambience, and the motivation of a whole department.

"He's not really an authority; he doesn't accomplish much."

Companies function on the basis of *explicit or implicit policies*. Even if they are not openly declared, these policies mark the company and the ambiance that is created. These policies determine the important points, the primary and secondary purposes as it were; they establish priorities. They influence the system and its functioning and, over and above this, the employees' perceptions.

"I'm working for the Americans and with these people, you're always left holding the bag."
"I like a small company better. You feel responsible and when you're doing things right one gets rewarded."
"When you are a civil servant you have nothing to fear."

Internal communication is part of the functioning process of the company. This is made obvious in the sense that there are communication programs and policies. In fact, communication is often double: there is official communication and unofficial communication, which answer to the system and its functioning or echo its characteristics.

"They don't tell us anything; we are kept in the dark."

Finally, the last element is less connected with its stable elements. These are the events, the factual elements, which will color the company positively or negatively in the eyes of the staff. These events can also determine the perception the individuals have of the company.

"They gave my boss the sack. A nice person. I'll never forget him."
"My boss had taken leave for the funeral of his father."

So, the company is a sum of characteristics, a totality of attributes that make up a system. Certain elements outweigh others and the distribution of these elements move constantly according to the events, the results, the persons, and the communication... These elements make the company into an incessantly moving system that is incessantly evaluated by its staff.

Depending on their fears, their aspirations, and their impressions, these employees have a certain perception of the company. This being the system within which he has to find his place, the employee continually evaluates the company. From eight to five – or in fact even longer, in his thoughts that is – the company constitutes his frame of reference.

The employee thus forms an image of the company that is consistent with these different elements. To some of them, the name of the company or the content of their work will be important whereas to others the factuality or the policy will be more important. The person himself determines these attentions, often unconsciously, by his aspirations, his models, and his fears.

Within this universe, it is thus possible to find distinct types of employees and mark their distinctive features. It is possible to do so, schematically, going from the employee's perfect attachment – and thus from his participation – to an absence of attachment and participation. Between these two extremes, we can observe various stages. Different things may also bring about these motivations and adhesions – the content of the work, the security and so forth. Without entering into the details of the various groups – the representativeness of which may vary depending on the company – we can present four typical profiles to illustrate our conception.

The *Egoists* are employees who are steered in their work by their own interests. These can be a search for prestige, for power, or they can also be things more closely related to their work such as competency or knowledge. These individuals are more or less attached to the company. They will generally be active but their activity is centered on themselves in the first place. The company benefits from it in a secondary or indirect way. The company itself also serves the employee's interests: his need for recognition, for example.

The *Claimants* are also self-centered. Their need for distinction has a more demanding tone. At the source of their demands lies the uncertainty created by their work or by the environment – their fellow workers, the content of the work and so on. Their participation is less important. They are less involved, in the sense that they will contribute less strongly to the cohesion of the company. They are claimants in the sense that their interests are in opposition with those of the company.

The "*Normatives*" too are marked by a sense of insecurity. Nevertheless, they lessen this feeling in a more passive or more responsible way. Their main aim is to have an employment because it is a reassuring situation or because employment is a sign of belonging, a norm. Hence, their involvement does not depend on their immediate interest or that of the company; they will act from a more normative point of view. Work is a 'routine' and must therefore be executed in a responsible way.

The *Participators* do their work in a relatively constructive way. These employees have developed a desire to advance themselves but also advance the company that employs them. According to these employees, the ideal work situation is the pursuit of a common goal. Hence, they are result-oriented without however frantically chasing after recognition. Their motto is 'evolvement'.

It goes without saying that all those different persons are not motivated by the same things and that we cannot address them in the same manner, just like companies address consumers in a targeted way.

Indeed, in view of the different elements that compose the companies and of the different profiles of the employees, it should be noticed that, even if there is dissatisfaction, the 'consumers' continue consuming their company, just like in ordinary consumption of products and services. This is due to the fact that the company and the employment represent frames of reference – or cultures – that are unique. I will try now to enumerate its specifics.

Frames of reference

The employee moves within a framework, within a culture that more or less agrees with him, to which he is more or less attached. So, this culture fundamentally differs from educational culture in the sense that *it can be challenged and can give cause for dissatisfaction*. One does not challenge one's life or all systems of reference such as one can challenge one's position within a company even if one's relation with work is more long-term than with a chocolate bar. The company does not influence the employee in the sense that it is not a mold in which the employee is shaped. This is indeed the eve of the 21st century. This means that the company is a complex world but also a relatively conscious element: to judge this frame of reference we need the human conscience.

That is why companies try to maximize the attachment and thus the participation and the motivation of their employees and try to meet with their aspirations. A motivational approach will allow to find which particular elements cause problems but also which benefits the employees have and adapt either its functioning or its communication or even its ambience.

"A satisfied employee is a motivated employee and a motivated employee is a productive employee."
"A satisfied consumer..."

Companies consist of groups of distinct individuals because people evolve and because the company develops. As a matter of fact, the change and the resistance against change cause many problems within the company, as it happens to be a unique culture: *it imposes change*. When a person changes cars, it is a more or less well-considered personal change. When a person changes colleagues, it generally is a surprise and, at worst, a disenchantment. This change and this choice are indeed imposed. It gives rise to a sense of uncertainty, which one has to overcome as quickly as possible, with whatever means.

In this system there are unexpected events – satisfactory or otherwise – that will 'shake up' the individual. The company culture is indeed *not a protective culture*, a frame of reference that will stabilize the individual. Compared with other frames of reference, this difference is due to the fact that the company is an environment that has to unite different interests and will thus be based on a compromise, as we will see further.

With respect to consumption, the companies again constitute a unique culture: in a certain sense, it is an *inverted consumption*, which should result in the fidelity of the consumer – the employee – since one does not change work as one changes brands of chewing gum. When an employee enters a company he knows little about it: he knows its name – the brand, the product – and little more. He has to trust the people who select him and take him on but who do not always have the same aim. The latter will think of stability and of development and productivity, whereas the former will think of productivity or of intelligence. Their common aim is to level the expectations in order to generate attachment and motivation.

Once in place, the employee will little by little discover the company that will bring him more or less satisfaction. We can however rest assured: the satisfaction is very often connected with the content of the work, which the employee can know before his recruitment. Nevertheless, it is after a certain time only that the complete system is revealed to the employee. So, this act of consumption if inverted and could be compared to the relation people have with their bank. One is a client because it is the nearest bank or because it is the one with whom one's parents are, and finally one finds many faults with it. At the same time one stays with it because one does not change banks like one changes brands of chewing gum.

"Is it better elsewhere?"
"It is such a mess when you want to change your code."
"I have an excellent contact with the manager but the personal banking department is run by incompetent people."
"I've already changed banks two years ago."

Loyalty is partly based on a *compromise*, that is to say the capacity the individual has to take a part of dissatisfaction, which allows a company full play up to the end of the line. So there is a part of reflection and a part of compromise. In this culture, one does not act individually and instinctively. It is a *much more 'civilized' culture* inasmuch as there is interaction but also because there is much at stake. At the same time, it is more coercive, for a majority of employees anyway, since it is based on compromise.

Which are the different contributions of a qualitative approach of the employees of a company?

— Measuring the degree of satisfaction and dissatisfaction and uncovering its actual causes.
— A motivational approach of the employees and of the company: not seeing the workers as executives, employees or academics, as men and women of a definite age, but understanding them from a different angle, that of their aspirations, of their outlook on work and on the company, and of their deep-down motivations.
— Beyond the stage of understanding, the stage of action: knowing where to act, how to direct and target the actions and the communication.

I would like to wind up this argument with an answer to certain critical readers who might have a different view of 'consumption' in the world of enterprise.

"Wouldn't it be more accurate to say that the companies consume their employees than otherwise?"

Certainly, in many cases. However, even if companies are 'heavy consumers' of employees, they do not always consume them in an appropriate way. We could indeed make some critical comments on this approach.

—   Companies make profiles – including psychological profiles – of the job-applicants. They allow for the deep-down motivations, for the personality and for the expectations of their future employees. They nonetheless restrict themselves in their motivational selection in the sense that it is impossible to consider all the particulars of the system within which the employee will move. Moreover, the system and the employee are forever changing and the selection does not yet include the prediction of the transformations of the company and of its employees.
—   Finally, the profiles typify candidates to the extreme – 'dynamic person' and so forth – and do not always take into account the company, the content of the work, the functioning et cetera.

Therefore, the consumption of employees is non-consumption, in the sense that it entails turnover of staff and failures. The ideal consumption will be that made by the employee, in the sense that if he, being in the system, consumes the company he is working for, he will do so because he likes to do so and show his loyalty: the ideal client, somehow or other. Therefore, why not try to seduce him, since only the employees' satisfaction will be synonymous with success.

After secondary school in her home province Limburg, **Gaby Siera** *went to Rotterdam and studied International Management; she liked the sound of it, she liked the marketing part, but looking back, she missed the human element. So she went on the road again, to Utrecht, and studied Anthropology. She found it interesting, but missed the stimulating creativity of marketing; evening classes filled that void.*

For her terminal project, Gaby went to South Africa where she could finally combine both her interests – people and marketing: she researched the different roles of Blacks and Whites in South African advertising.

In 1997, Gaby Siera joined the staff at Censydiam. She has become a senior researcher in the Netherlands and occasionally supervises coaching courses at Censydiam Germany.

Since her stay in South Africa, Gaby likes to discover the world. This summer, for example, she went to Syria and Jordan, and as diving is her hobby, she combines plunging in the sea with immersing in new cultures.

Advertising in the Rainbow Nation

A pot of gold at the end of the rainbow

South Africa, the land that did the Dutch language the dubious honor of making the word apartheid world-famous. The land President Mandela gave the name of Rainbow Nation because of its multiplicity of population groups. South Africa, the most recent democracy at the very end — or at the beginning — of a continent where for many of the inhabitants surviving is literally the most important daily occupation. South Africa, the nation upon which the whole world's attention is fixed and which one hopes will set an example to all other African nations. South Africa, a land where despair and hopes, peace and violence, poverty and wealth struggle for priority every day. South Africa, an intriguing, resilient land with a zest for living, a land that grips you and never lets you go, a land that commands respect and that, as time goes by, shows you things that remained invisible when you first arrived...

"Hey, whitey," is one of the first greetings I hear when I stroll through the center of what used to be a 'coloured' South African neighborhood. Only when I had moved on a few steps, it came to me that I was meant. I happened to be the only white around — something which hardly ever happens in the Netherlands. I turn around and with the that strange feeling of pride that you can have as an outsider living in the country — apparently, I am more integrated than I thought — I smile broadly and return the greeting. Deep down I chuckle and oblivious to the fact that I have just been abused I continue my way through this country in black-and-white.

Advertising as a cultural system

I wonder how I, as a white woman coming from a country with a majority of whites, can get more insight into the relations between the black and white populations in this country. Reading books, talking with South Africans, observing people? All the means that come to the mind of an anthropologist — and probably to that of a non-anthropologist, too. But there is another instrument you can come upon everywhere, an instrument you cannot avoid, and gives you an easily accessible, profound and inviting insight into the values that play a role in the relations between blacks and whites: looking at advertisements.

Indeed, advertising can be seen as a projection of the values and norms of its devisers and producers, since they are part of that society. Advertising is a historically transmitted pattern of meanings embodied in symbols by the means of which men communicate, perpetuate, and develop their knowledge about the attitudes toward life. Advertising is, as it were, a mirror of symbols and therefore a mirror of the values that are important in the society in which the advertisements are made. It is a model of, as well as a model for reality. It is an idealized and manipulated reality. When we strip advertising of its glitter and glamour and look at the real norms and values it represents we can get an insight into the way on which one — in this case — puts a meaning on the relations between black and white people in South Africa.

Watching TV, sprawled in my easy chair

That is how I spend a large part of my time in South Africa: lying in front of the TV, with the remote control of the VCR in one hand and the remote control of the TV in my other and leafing through all kinds of magazines, just not to miss a single multiracial commercial or advertisement. Zapping my way through the South African media...

First, we have to divide the multiracial advertisements — adverts in which black as well as white models appear — into interactive and non-interactive messages. In the interactive ads we see black and white people actually communicating with each other or, at least, see them at the same time and in the same space. Advertising agents see non-interactive messages as an excellent means to resolve the tricky problem of whether they should make multiracial advertising or not in a diplomatic way. The non-interactive messages are characterized by the fact that black as well as white people do appear but do not – or are not able to – interact. Think for example of isolated shots or photos with either black or white people. They are as it were disconnected elements that are put together on one page or in one movie. Thus the consumer sees people with a different skin color together in one advertisement but does not see them having – or being able to have – contact with each other.

However, observing the circumstances in which the dichotomy is used is more interesting than the dichotomy itself. So it is interesting to see, for example, that non-interactive advertising is most particularly used for family situations. Instead of a multiracial family, we see a black and a white family by turns.

In many interactive multiracial ads, children play an important role. As children are unburdened with the apartheid of the past and full of the candor, the innocent self-assurance, and the openness that is typical for them, they form an ideal overture to relations between blacks and whites. In the new South Africa, it is easier to accept that black and white children play together or go to together – and in fact they do. There is a snag, of course. A manufacturer of copiers has found it out to his cost when the following Saint Valentine's Day commercial went on the air.

> A small white boy is playing in the factory where his father works. In his hand, he has a drawing of a big heart transfixed with an arrow. With the copier in his father's office, he makes numerous copies of his drawing. The following day we see the little boy running in the schoolyard with a batch of drawings in his hand. All the girls – black and white – get a drawing except for one of the black girls. Although it was clear that the boy did not disregard her deliberately, the commercial provoked a storm of protest. The producer was compelled to adapt the commercial. In the new version, all the girls without exception get a drawing.

It is also notable that in commercials black people play a wider range of roles than whites. The most common roles for whites are limited to their so-called yuppie role – the visibly successful businessman or woman – the role of friends, the role within domestic or family matters, and the role of 'model as model' – the model as showcase for the product such as in fashion photography. Next to them, black people fill the parts of sportsmen, artists, or workers. Showing sportsmen and artists is also a safe way to show the talents of black people. We are indeed dealing here with a small group of people who are exceptionally talented and therefore hardly threatening to the established order. Artists and sportsmen form as it were a world in itself outside the everyday world. The role of worker is a so-called typically black trade. In the time of apartheid, black people did the physically heavy and low paid work. Whereas I sporadically found an advertisement with whites in a black profession, ads with blacks in a traditionally white profession were almost nonexistent. Advertisers try to avoid the black stereotype as much as possible by mingling black and white in typically black professions. Not showing black people – or making them less visible – in typically white professions however denies them admission to the domain of the whites. Except for the modern executive – who is in any case the symbol of the modern, Western-oriented, new South Africa, and therefore should be black – black people are absent from the white professions.

But what about the multiracial groups as they appear in advertising? For the most part, they are groups in which blacks and whites are equally divided. The relation between black and white, too, is equal: nobody is the boss; it is one great party for everybody. In the main, the basis of such a relation is a group of friends or colleagues.

Leafing and zapping, I come upon an interesting phenomenon. Everyone in this country feels strongly about political correctness. If they do not represent black and white people as partners of equal value, advertising executives seem to be afraid of being reproached with being people who live in the past and want to go back to the times of apartheid. An underdog situation in which a black person is the dupe is totally unacceptable, especially if it turns out that the white person has the upper hand. The reverse however, an underdog situation in which the white person comes off worst, is great fun. By choosing stereotypical white people one avoids that white South Africans identify with the losers and protest: they are white people with which one does not want to identify anyway – at least not I. And you? Want to join me watching?

> A white journalist – obviously the 'open sandals and woolen socks developing aid type' – is sitting in the middle of the bush typing up his report. In the same room sits an imposing black man who watches silently. The journalist says to the black man in a pedantic tone: "Look, push button and types. Easy, uh?" When he has finally finished his paper, he asks the black man the way to the post office. "Post office?" The man, still silent, points at a sign that says that the post office is thirty miles away. Then he gets up and asks: "Why don't you fax it?" When they are standing at the fax machine, he says, in the same pedantic tone as the journalist: "Look, push button and faxes. Easy, uh?"

The following commercial – by a provider of mobile telephony – is one of my series of 'absolute favorites.'

> An old black man, who looks very neat, is selling souvenirs made from iron wire at the side of the road. At a certain point, a fast red car stops. Its occupants are a rather unsavory-looking white man and his quite uncomely girl friend. She is obviously charmed by the souvenirs. While she is looking over them at length, the white man says to the black with a supercilious look and in a belittling tone that must make clear that he speaks Zulu fluently: "Yebo gogo." This means in fact "Hello, granny." Yet, "yebo" is not a greeting but an answer to a greeting and "gogo" means "grandmother" but is insulting when you speak to an old woman you are not acquainted with. In short, he is making a fool of himself. Meantime, they find out that the souvenirs cost 100 rand a piece and the white man finds that it is too much for "a piece of scrap iron." He wants to get back in his car and drive off. Then we see his car keys in the ignition and, of course, the doors are locked. The old black man produces his mobile phone

and calls the AA. In the last shot, we see the white man and his girl friend drive away. Their car is crammed with iron-wire souvenirs.

More interesting still than the people who play a role in advertisements is the setting in which they are put. There is a notable absence of multiracial advertisements set in private rooms. In adverts blacks and whites meet on the shop floor, in a bar, on the sports field, in the street, in the park, they meet everywhere except at each other's homes or under circumstances that are connected with their personal family circles or circles of friends. In sum, coming together in public places is one thing, in the private sphere another; this is clearly a little bit too close. As one must not look for what is there but for what is not there, this is not immediately obvious. With children, again, it seems to be easier. They can go visit each other and play together with a white or a black mother, watching the emergence of a new South Africa with a contented smile.

Aside from adverts filled with black and white people, a multicolored parade of very Western-oriented ads files past my eyes. Cities with the American touch, the Caribbean Sea filled with white cabin cruisers and long-legged beauties galore. Western values and norms leap forward from magazines and television. With the importation of a Western lifestyle, the success, the richness, the power, and the worldly pleasures of the West are imported instinctively. It is to be noted that, these days, adverts in the West itself often appeal to a 'living life to the max' feeling. They search for an exciting escape from the relatively structured and regulated life. In South Africa, on the other hand, they are fed up for the moment with living 'to the max.' Western-oriented advertising capitalizes more on the quality of life and the feeling of security and certainty the West has to offer. Slogans such as "More than one hundred thousand people use this product whose recipe has not been changed since 1880" or "Number one in America and Europe" must win the South African consumers over. Its Western counterpart would certainly think that such a product has a character too large to be a fitting expression of its unique, individual, and especially very individual, unpredictable identity.

Advertising in South Africa

Squinting after all those hours of watching TV and curious about the people behind those commercials, I try to make appointments with South African advertising executives. It worked wonderfully well. Many are willing to allow me a glimpse behind the scenes.

By that time, it seemed to me that advertising in South Africa was not an easy matter. Aside from the fact that, in my eyes, making a good advert is difficult in any case, you have to consider the susceptibilities in this country. When I hear the many definitions with which they try to describe the so-called new target group, the 35 million black consumers who appeared out of nothingness, it proves that advertising people themselves have problems with it. Here are the seven definitions I found. Any suggestions as to further additions will be gratefully received.

— The Black Market. It refers specifically to the black consumers. Their white counterparts form the 'White Market.' There is a problem here with the 'coloured' consumers — a group that as far as skin color goes falls between white and black and at the time of apartheid had a middle position: more rights than black people and less than the whites. Where do they stand now? Most advertisers think that this group is part of the 'black market,' as their buying behavior shows more similarities with it.

— The Non-white Market. The same group, in fact, as the 'black market' but named from a different perspective. Here also the 'coloured' population causes a problem: it is non-white, too, and rather belongs to the black South African group than to the white group.

— The African Market. The African market comprises all (black) South Africans and strongly refers to the traditional tribal sense of the black population.

— The Main Market. The fact that 80% of the total population is black is quite something. Although they are not on the same level with the whites as regards their income, this group can no longer be ignored.

— The Majority Market. A somewhat more functional description of the same target group. In this case, the white consumer is part of the 'Minority Market.'

— The Historically Disadvantaged Market. This is political correctness at its best! These are all the people who in the past have had a subordinate part and have been disadvantaged. Not only black and 'coloured' people but the women and the disabled are part of this group.

— The Imaginary Market. There is no group of consumers of just blacks or just whites, a homogeneous group whose needs would be determined by the color of their skin.

The description of a 'Black Market' is the one the trade journals and the marketing manuals generally use. South African advertising people are evidently conscious of the fact that they are not dealing with a homogeneous group of black consumers but it is easier to give the group one single name. Yet, to get away from this classification according to skin color and surely also to get a more detailed insight into the different target groups, they have been looking for new classifications. The Living Standards Measure (LSM) is one of the better known. On the basis of 13 variables — among which the possession of an icebox, TV and so on, where one does one's shopping, whether one lives in an urban or rural area and disposes of water and electricity — the South African population has been divided into eight groups. Although skin color is part of the model, the five first groups appear to be mainly black; white is hardly noticeable. Groups 7 and 8 are predominantly white with just a little drop of black. Meeting with the above-mentioned criteria is still too strongly associated with the rights and duties South African citizens had during apartheid. It is still too early to see an actual shift.

All that zapping and leafing has made me nod off. I dreamed that I — as an explorer of a contemporary world, as a modern Jan van Riebeeck, — discovered a new South Africa and wished to get to know the reality of South Africa and understand it with the eyes of all the inhabitants of this country... Is this not a fine task in store for researchers? A classification based on motivations is — in my eyes — the only way to get away from a black and white division. Motivation indeed passes by external and — to a certain extent — sociodemographic characteristics. I should not forget that I wanted to take you on a zapping tour of the South African advertising world. Back to reality, wake up!

Although the South African advertising business is known as male and pale, most advertising agencies are up and about recruiting black colleagues. Whereas in adverts black people, contrary to whites, fairly often play the creative (artistic) roles, I have encountered few black people in the creative departments of the advertising agencies; black people are sooner employed in customer-oriented services. South Africans tell me that this is due to the fact that they are more visible there and that the bureau wants to make a good impression on the outside world. Well, maybe. But they raised another interesting question, the idea that black creative people would be better at designing advertising for black people and whites for whites. What about advertising for women, children, and senior citizens then? To me, an open outlook, which stems from a real and sincere wish to get to know and understand the consumers through and through and to get an insight into their motivations and desires, seems more inspiring and more flexible – and cheaper – than recruiting people from every single population group. There are no less than eight black and two white population groups, and then we do not even talk about the internal differences within these groups.

I do not want to give the impression that South African advertising people would be inconsiderate, or racist. It is, quite contrary, a line of business that is in for challenging, stimulating but also difficult and uncertain times. The bounds have still to be found and this asks for creative solutions.

As there was, during the times of apartheid, a fairly strict separation between black and white media, one could allow oneself to communicate products that were meant for black as well as for white consumers through separate channels. The same commercial was shot twice, for example, one time with a black model and once more with a white, and could later be distributed through white and black-oriented media.

> A well-know brand of soap segmented its market into a white and a black target group. The commercial aiming at the white target group shows a white woman lying in a bath full of foam, and singing. Her husband walks into the bathroom. She is startled and stops singing. "Feel good and feel free with this soap!" In the commercial for black consumers we also see a singing women – a black woman in this case. However, it is not her husband who walks into the bathroom, but her child. The woman is not startled, on the contrary, she goes on singing cheerfully, along with her child.

The reaction of a black staff member at an advertising agency was scathing: a poor and preposterous commercial suggesting that among black people it is prohibited to enter the bathroom when one's wife is taking a bath. Belittling at that, as it suggests that different commercials should be made for the different groups. A white staff member – at a different agency – spoke well of it: it takes into consideration the cultural differences of the two target groups.

Now that the separation of the black and white media diminishes and everyone has access to all media, the odds are that the same consumer will see both commercials. The challenge for the advertising people to make appealing multiracial adverts and commercials whenever they want to address white as well as black consumers. Every advertising executive however admits using different strategies to avoid making multiracial adverts. Animals – South African animals – are especially popular stand-ins for people. South Africa has an extensive and appealing animal world which can symbolize the country. Different species can embody the different values one wants to appeal to. Using national sports heroes is another interesting option to avoid an interracial discussion. Through his or her achievements, the national sports hero surpasses the ordinary man and woman in the street. He and – to a lesser degree – she live in their own world in which only performance counts and not one's origin.

Black-and-white: symbol for the new South Africa

The things you learn from looking intensively at advertising! If you are on holiday and have not much time to spare but want to learn something about the prevailing norms and values in your vacation spot, shut yourself in your hotel room and watch television. I happen to have focused on the relations between black and white in South Africa but to get general knowledge about a culture too, advertising is an easily accessible and, with a bit of luck, an engaging and entertaining source of information. Last but not least, do not forget to look for what is... not there.

The relation between blacks and whites in South African commercials is not simply a relation between people but a symbol of the new avenue South Africa has taken. It is a relation that can be a symbol of many values. Making interactive multiracial advertising goes beyond political correctness. The symbolic value of this relation can, just like any other symbol, be used in combination with other settings and other characters to communicate certain values. It is a relation that, from its historical pregnancy, is recognized and understood by everyone in South Africa.

Thus, the relation between blacks and whites in advertising wants to symbolize a contemporary spirit, courage, and self-assurance; the interpretation of a feeling that one leads the way and distances oneself from accepted values and norms: this is a more progressive way of using the symbol of black-and-white. The relation between black and white can also stand for a feeling of friendship, acceptance, and cooperation: thus, it represents the more constructive side of the new South Africa. Yet, black and white can also stand for uncertainty, anxiety, and a feeling of powerlessness. It is a strong and very powerful symbol. It is a symbol that rouses great emotion and thus receives much attention because of which the perception around the subject of the advertisement is in danger of being overlooked.

Yet, I have seen quite a number of appealing and engaging adverts in which the relations between black and white are used in a stimulating and purposeful way. In these cases, South African advertising people have not only succeeded in using the symbolic value of black and white in a positive way but also offered both groups the possibility to get acquainted in an approachable and engaging way and accept each other. In my eyes, indeed, the latter is an important responsibility for an industry that has so much power to decide upon the information we get through the media every day.

Having finished my thumbing through magazines and zapping the TV channels, in South Africa at least, I realize that the relations between blacks and whites as it is represented by South African advertising appear to be the same – on a smaller scale – as in my own country, the Netherlands. Is it not so that we see many representatives of our Turkish, Moroccan, Surinamese or Antillean communities in our advertising? And in what roles? And how does that come across with the Dutch? No idea! Those are the shortcomings of the anthropologist: more observant of foreign things than of what is going on in one's own country. Here at home, too, I should lie down on the couch with the remote control of the video recorder in one hand and the remote control of the TV in the other...

Martine Roefflaer *began her career as a psychotherapist, specializing in problems with upbringing.*

Since 1988, she has been active in the field of Qualitative Diagnostic Research at Censydiam. She is an expert in Kids and Teens Market Research. The reflection of her knowledge and experiences in different European countries can be found in "Kids and Teens Marketing", which is currently in preparation at Censydiam for Kids Antwerp.

Martine is also a welcome guest speaker at international meetings and congresses where she propagates her – and our – views on life stage marketing and integrating kids, teens, and adult marketing.

The world upside down? The end of target marketing? You can read all about it in the following paper. It was first communicated on the occasion of the New Parenthood Movement day at the Antwerp... zoo, which does not necessarily imply a reference to Durrell's "Family and Other Animals."

The new parenthood movement

A world upside down

Sometimes we hear people of an older generation complain that "there are no children anymore." They might well be right. The dependent "mother's child" is losing ground.

You have to admit that it is not surprising that the older generation sometimes frowns when they see how parents and children relate to each other these days. It must be like taking a walk at the other side of Alice's mirror or in a Never-Never Land come true.

I shall give you some examples:

— When we were children, we accompanied our parents wherever <u>they</u> went. Nowadays, children want to go somewhere and their parents can come along, too — or stay home... alone.
— We used to play with toys. Our own children play with real things from the adult world like T.V., video, CD player, CD-ROM, and computers.
— When we were young, the friends we used to play with were the children of our parents' friends. Now, parents become friends with the parents of their children's friends.
— Our parents taught us how to ride a bike, how to swim, they helped us with our homework. Nowadays, children teach their parents how to play computer games and how to use in-line skates.
— When we first opened an account at the bank, we asked our parents for advice and ended up taking an account at the same bank they were with. These days, young adults advise their parents to change banks and join the bank *they* chose.

In other words, children take the lead; parents have to keep up with them. What is going on?

We are in a period of transition

The children of today are clearly different, and not only because they play computer games or watch more television.

Children of today are different because they have a different place in the family structure and in society in general. Today, at the end of the 20th century, children become "different" because the traditional, middle-class family structure becomes less important.

Children break away from family ties much sooner. They find themselves in a peer group, in the group of other children, much earlier. In market research, we see that the age at which the peer group is just as important a reference as the family becomes increasingly lower. Whereas some years ago the limit was nine, we now see that it has shifted to eight or even seven. The time that the child is rooted in its family becomes shorter and the moment when the peer group becomes determinant, comes sooner.

The ideal way of bringing up children is no longer obvious these days. Parents also have to redefine their role. We are in a period of transition.

Up to now, three clearly distinct family models existed

During nine years of research in the market for kids and youngsters, we were able to observe the shifts in family culture and upbringing.

While studying the needs of parents and children — be it in a marketing context — we noticed that for bringing up children, parents could choose from three main strategies. We refer to these three variants with the terms *mothering, gatekeeping,* and *sharing.*

The first model is the most traditional, the closed family model. The latter is the most modern and, historically speaking, the most "progressive"and recent model.

The "mothering" family

The "mothering" family comes closest to the traditional, middle-class family. This family is a typically closed private sphere, a safe home where the child is far away from the dangerous world outside. In this family structure, the mother can guarantee her child a real childhood.

In "mothering" families, roles are divided traditionally. Father goes out to work, mother stays home and looks after the kids. The "mothering" mother does not really picture herself as a woman, but rather as mother. When she introduces herself to others, she exclusively defines herself in relation to her children. She would be nobody without her children; she needs them to function. When she talks to other women, she talks about the children.

For this type of mother, a child is the ultimate "small" and "dependent" being, which needs care and help. She appreciates all signals indicating that the child needs care. For instance: she will not at all mind when her child is covered in chocolate, because then she can wash it and pamper it. She is the one who will hold the wash cloth. This same mother will continue to make her children's sandwiches for a long time, will accompany them to the toilet, and will continue to pour their milk... This mother's children get lots of toys. Within the world of toys, they get a lot of autonomy, as long as everything happens within the boundaries of the family, safely tied to mommy's apron strings.

The "gatekeeping" mother

The "gatekeeping" mother also pays a lot of attention to her children, but this attention results from a different attitude.

She does not really care for the children excessively or pamper them; she mainly keeps an eye on them. Whereas the mothering mother will look for reasons to take care of the children, the "gatekeeping mother" will adopt an opposite, prevention-minded attitude. She prefers things to run as smoothly as possible. The less trouble, the better. In her approach, order and control occupy center stage. She will rather try to prevent that her children will be covered in chocolate. Everything has to be – and to remain – in tip-top order. This mother is often very sensitive to norms. She does not only want to keep everything under control; she also wants the outside world to think she effectively does.

"Gatekeeping" mothers do not want to keep their children small, as the "mothering mother" does, but they do not simply give it autonomy either. Children have to grow up, but in an organised manner, according to plan. Everything in due time. At four, they can make their own sandwiches; at 12, they can go to the shop alone; at 16, go to a party by bike. This mother rears her children towards autonomy, step by step.

The "sharing mother"

The "sharing" mother is only mother in part. She is a part-time mother, and a part-time woman. She definitely thinks that there is more to life than motherhood. She also has her own life, apart from the children. She usually goes out to work, and makes full use of day nursery facilities. When she is among friends, she will talk about other things besides the children, about things that interest her as a woman. Of these three women, the "sharing mother" is the most emancipated. The freedom that she grants herself results in the fact that she finds that her role should not necessarily differ from the role of the father. Hence, we could just as well talk about a "sharing father" or a "sharing couple."

For the "sharing" mother, a child is not small at all or, by definition, in need of help. She prefers to see her children as being independent and she gives them autonomy as much and as soon as possible. She likes her children to be able to do things, to take responsibility. Whereas the "mothering mother" prefers her children to play at home, the "sharing" mother likes her children to go out and play with their friends.
The "sharing model" does not only have a liberated vision of women, but also of children. Sharing parents consider their children to be their equals. There is no more hierarchy. You can talk to children as if they were adults.

Basically, "sharing" is "time-sharing." The parents divide their time between themselves and the children, and contemporary family life merely consists of a number of moments, of well-defined periods during which the family members are together and "do something together."

"Sharing" parents highly appreciate these periods of being together. They will cherish these moments and they will try to do things together as often as possible, to have the feeling that there is a true bond.

Stereotypes

Obviously, these three models are stereotypes. In reality, you will never find them as such. They rather come in mixed forms, although one of the three types will usually dominate in real life. In most Western countries, we notice that the dominance of one model emerges. Our practical experience has taught us that the sharing model, for instance, dominates the UK, whereas German mothers tend to apply a gatekeeping strategy. In

Southern countries, the mothering pattern is quite dominant: "la mamma" is life itself — she is as important as "la Madonna."

The new meaning of the child is also a result of the rise of the "sharing" model

It is quite important however that, everywhere around us, we notice an evolution from the more family-related models such as mothering and gatekeeping, to the rather low-profile family "sharing" model. The emancipation of women and the reshuffle of the traditional role patterns definitely contribute to this evolution.

When the family as a "safe haven" loses ground to the peer group, this is mainly caused by the rise of the sharing model. Children from these families wind up in childcare much sooner, or find themselves among "peers", and participate in all sorts of activities outside of school and in clubs.

Therefore, children become preadolescents very rapidly: children can no longer enjoy a carefree childhood to the fullest, but fairly soon have to assume responsibility, while still being children.

Who is this new parent?

Yet, the new parents of today are different from the "sharing" parents. The "new parent" is a further evolution of the sharing parent, a next step in the evolution. The new parent does not consider parenthood as "part of life," like the sharing parent, who thinks, "work eight hours, be a parent for four." The new parent considers it an important phase in life. For instance, after building a relationship, after building a house, after building up a career, there is the phase of having children. The new parent really wants to make the best of this new phase, too.

However, things are not always easy for the new parent. They experience the drawbacks of the sharing model.

— The new parents constantly have the feeling that they do not spend enough time with their children. Quite often, both parents work and have the feeling that they need to catch up on so many things.
— After all, parents increasingly have the feeling that they lose touch with

their children.

— In this, the new parent strongly experiences the disadvantages of the "sharing relationship." The essence of this modern way of being together is that it simply is a "poor family life." The family experience merely consists of loose arrangements between family members, of separate moments, whereas for the rest, everybody does his own thing. The "sharing parents" claim a lot of autonomy for themselves and, for the same reason, stimulate their children's autonomy. Consequently, parent and child are drifting apart and become strangers to each other.

— Being alienated from one's child is also the result of other, external, factors. The giant leap of the media and of technology leads to an "accelerated" generation gap. The world becomes increasingly complex and the gap between the world of the parents and the world of the children seems to become bigger and bigger.

— Children also seem to be less ready to be educated, less receptive to their parents' authority. This is a result of being cut loose so soon. The pressure from the peer group becomes increasingly strong.

— Parents worry about the extreme way in which children are confronted with the harsh adult world. The essence of the new situation of the parents is that they cannot guarantee their children to prolong their childhood. At a very early age, children are confronted with the harsh world of adults, which they continue to view from a child's perspective.

What can you do, as a parent, when your children want to watch "Rescue 911"? Or when they want to empty their piggy bank and give it to "Help Kosovo"? Or when they refuse to eat their food, pretending it is "full of dioxin" though mother claims that she bought it from a "safe butcher"?

Therefore, new parents have the feeling of losing control over there lives and contact with their children.

Parents no longer think "never mind..." as sharing parents do, but try to pick up the thread in various ways. They look for all sorts of means and channels to enable them to talk to their children, to get a part of their life with the children back under control...

These parents perceive "getting control" differently from the previous types.

Yesterday, one used to speak about the children's phases of development; now they focus on those of the parents. People refer to parents with babies, parents with young children, parents with adolescents... All these phases require a different form of relationship between parents and children. The new parents have the feeling that they have to grow through these new phases, that they have to live up to things, that they have to develop, to mature. Parents discover themselves through having children. Having children means discovering yourself, having children means growing up.

The new parent does feel responsible for the upbringing of her or his child, but it is a different form of responsibility. The new form of assuming responsibility for the children has changed from protecting and controlling to showing the way. They feel that children can assume some responsibility, but the new parent constantly wonders how far this responsibility should stretch. Parents no longer think, "never mind," but try to take things in hand again, in all sorts of ways.

There is a lot of vagueness… but a new model is in the making

Parents no longer know how far they should let a child's autonomy go. The future is the great unknown. In the old days, children had to become lawyers or doctors, but nothing is clear these days.

The problem today is that parents no longer have clear answers, no clear solutions. Nobody tells them how they should do it. Educational models that were used for their own upbringing no longer meet the changed social model of today. The appropriate model needs to be completed: it is a search, and the solution is still in the making.

Parents decide to found parents' associations to handle the problem together, to exchange experiences, and to find guidelines for relating with their children. Parenting websites shoot up like mushrooms. The corporate world realises the young parents' need for information. Pampers, for instance, has its own very exhaustive website, where parents can read articles, chat with each other and with specialists — such as Dr. Brazzelton, an American educational guru who has his agony column on the site.

Society in general, but marketing to kids, too, should adapt to these changing needs

These growing needs in the recent development of families obviously have their impact on marketing to kids.

- The new parent is continuously looking for a positive contact with his children, and willing to invest a lot in it. Together with his children, he wants to explore new things. We can consider the new parent as a new consumer who has an enormous openness towards new products, which he wants to discover together with his children. It is important not to concentrate too much on "kids-only" products but to create products which can appeal to kids as well as to adult consumers.
- The new family has, and this is not different from the sharing family, a need for family moments, for "family tokens," around which the members of the family can unite. It is about creating special places, occasions, special products that offer the family the chance of being a real family — for example, re-inventing classics like "Star Wars." Marketing can fill a void there. It can create moments and products that enable a family feeling.
- The difference with this family is that anything that helps the parents to close the gap between parents and children is appropriate. Anything that forms a good compromise between innovation and traditional support, between children and parents is interesting. The recent success of retro and traditional toys is not surprising. Toys associating games and education (edutainment) are more popular than ever. They associate games and education, give the parents the feeling that they still can control, and understand the situation: new Lego concepts with microchips, sensors and "intelligent" material, and so on. Retro and "edutainment" is an excellent mix to ease the parental fear for a gap that is too big, a child that is too different, in a world that is too complex. It makes the inhuman world, in which, according to parents, a child has to live, more human. It acts as a compensation for the proscribed childishness, and as a closing of the gap between parents and children.

The positive side of this evolution

The positive side of this evolution is that having children has an indisputable educational effect on the new parent. It is an important and beautiful phase in life, it helps to put things into perspective, and it helps personal development.

Sigrid Jansen *studied Communication Management in The Hague and Management and Organization at the University of Utrecht, where she wrote her final dissertation on quality care and customer relations.*

One of her first assignments as metrical researcher at Censydiam Netherlands was to measure customer satisfaction at a bank. Since then, she has researched soft drinks, beer, and the potential of a new medicine against asthma in the Netherlands, and a tobacco product in Germany and India.

Her recreational interests range from rowing to drawing and painting. And what about superstition? Sigrid is a member of the editorial staff of a publication for former pupils of the The Hague InterCollege which is published under the rather "airy" title of Luchtkastelen (Castles in Spain). Sigrid is not really superstitious and does not build castles in the air; she is above all that.

If you want to find out more, just try to enter the castle... if you dare!

Walking under ladders and spilling salt ...
Superstition and popular belief

It is Wednesday, May 7, not exactly an exceptional day. The alarm is jangling and I wake up with a start. Snippets of a dream still wander in my mind. A strange horse ran right through the house during the night. A horse means dying, important news arriving, or it can refer to mixing with the wrong people. While I lie thinking about that, it dawns to me that it is going to be a busy day at Censydiam. I jump out of bed and immediately realize that I have got out on the wrong side.

Downstairs, at the kitchen table, I eat two slices of bread and drink a glass of milk. I look up the lottery numbers in the paper. My number, ending in 84, is not among the winners. And those are my lucky numbers, if you please! I say bye to the cat and walk out of the door. The cat is black but no, he has never brought me bad luck.

Speaking of cats, it is raining cats and dogs. I quickly enter our office building, with my opened umbrella, though I know it brings bad luck. Well, let us calmly wait and see.

First, a quick cup of coffee in the canteen. I bump into Jolanda who unfortunately has dropped a glass while emptying the dishwasher. Rini, who just came in, immediately says that broken glass will bring good luck.

Another colleague tells me that in a fortnight she goes on vacation to France. She has been lucky and her camping trips were never spoiled by bad weather. Her remark is followed by a knock on the wooden table. I tell her that I shall keep my fingers crossed for her.

In the morning, many people are milling around in the canteen at Censydiam. I run into a pregnant colleague. On her tummy, she wears a little tintinnabulum that must prepare her baby for its life in the 'external' world.

The bunch of flowers on the reception desk comprises several narcissuses. One does point directly at the incoming visitors. Just to be sure, I shift it a little. Imagine some of our clients knowing that a narcissus pointing towards you brings bad luck. Not a very promising introduction.

Arriving at my workplace, my roommate Ben calls the reception to get a reference number for a fax. He has to send an important proposal to a client this morning. He hangs up and says, 'Gee! I've got number 13!'

Just the first hours of an ordinary day. I realize that during these few hours I have been confronted several times with my own superstitions. The more I think about it, the more I see that superstition is still well established in our everyday life.

What exactly is superstition?

There are innumerable forms of behavior that we can give the name of superstition. Think of 'lucky pieces' such as the coins on bracelets or the little dolls hanging from the rearview mirrors. Lighting a candle for a beloved one can also be rated among superstition. Or the belief among actors that a bad dress rehearsal promises an immense success for the opening performance. Friends of mine read their horoscope every week but tell me that they do it just for fun. And I myself cross my fingers as a friend goes in for an exam.

What exactly is superstition? *Superstition is the belief that an object, an action, or a circumstance not logically related to a course of events will influence its outcome. This belief is based on the idea that there is more than we can rationally explain.*

A closer look at 'there is more than we can rationally explain'

At the basis, there is the belief that there is more than our existence on this earth. We cannot explain everything: there is more than we, humans, can understand. To gain control of the inexplicable, we fill it in. Not always very rationally. But do we always think rationally, anyway? Certain behavior is inspired by our emotions. We cannot explain, for example, why we perform a certain action or are convinced of a certain idea.

Hence, we find people who are convinced that our fate is written in the stars. Others are convinced that alien people live in outer space and have been visiting us on Earth to see how we live. The circles they leave in our grain fields would be proof of that. Still others think that – good as well as bad – spirits wander around and influence our lives.

A closer look at 'influences its outcome'

We know indeed that certain forces are at work. This is a fact. It is important then to find a way in which to deal with this fact. By arranging one's life in a certain way, one can try to limit the influence of higher powers. Superstition gives something to hold on to. It prescribes certain acts to deal with life in the most positive way possible, i.e. that we can get as many chances out of life as possible and be confronted with the least possible mischance. The fact is however that fate sometimes decides; there are limitations.

Different names for the same thing

Superstition comes in different forms. It is impossible to draw a clear line between what is superstition and what is not. Nobody wants to hear that he or she is superstitious. Superstition has a negative undertone. There is no proof that there is any truth in superstition and if you happen to believe in it, you are considered odd or unsure.

The negative flavor of superstition comes from the choice of the term in the first place. In English, the word 'superstition' has a supernatural ring; it is something 'above' ordinary life. The German word is 'Aberglauben' and the Dutch 'bijgeloof'. They indicate that it is a belief 'apart from' real belief. They connote that superstition is an incomplete, an imperfect outlook on life, that it is incidental.

Because of the negative image it calls forth, nobody wants to practice superstition. Hence the boundary between superstition and belief is a subjective one. Nobody wants to hear the things he is convinced of being true belief described as superstition. Still, many things are considered superstition or based on superstition. Think of folktales, myths, legends, religious tales, astrology, satanic verses, sorcery, charlatanism, dream interpretation, horoscopes, palmistry, and acupuncture.

Popular belief

The term popular belief is closest to what we call superstition. Popular belief is often based on old myths and sagas that contain a certain moral. Good and evil play an important role in popular belief. Good and evil are personified in characters such as Santa Claus and the devil.

We can often pinpoint the origin of folk tales to particular regions or families. The Loch Ness Monster is a good example. There are also tales about certain houses that are haunted by the spirits of dead.

Everyone is superstitious…

Although the majority of Europeans will say that they "do not really bother with superstition," we are confronted with it every day. Superstition has deep roots in European history. Why is it then that superstition is commonly negated? There are many reasons for it. Many superstitious acts are no longer noticed or recognized as superstitious. Moreover, superstition goes under different names and is not always identified as such.

… but not all to the same extent

The extent to which one is involved with superstition is up to the person itself. Do we actually believe in influencing our good luck or do we doubt it? Whereas some seriously believe that tossing a coin into a well will make a wish come true, others attach little importance to it. Some will make jokes about a four-leaf clover, others will rather be safe than sorry and just make sure.

In certain cultures or subcultures superstition is of the order of the day

Superstition is also connected with certain cultures or subcultures. Certain cultures are known for the many rituals they follow. Think of voodoo or of the rain dances in Africa. Here we will restrict ourselves to the European culture.

When we zoom in on the different subcultures, we find that fishermen, actors, gamblers and sporting people are more superstitious than others. At certain moments, these groups need to make special efforts and – in addition to that – they are dependent on others or other things: on the quantity of fish, on the public, on being able to memorize their text in a few days, on their partners, on just that particular moment in the Olympics. These moments are unpredictable and, in these critical situations, one is tempted to bear a helping hand to luck.

Where does superstition stem from?
Traces in history.

Who has invented that misfortune will befall you when you walk under a ladder? Or that you may kiss anyone under a mistletoe? Or that you may never put a contract on a bed lest it becomes a... sleeping contract?

We know the background of many of these tales. The original meaning of superstitious acts however has been lost. In many cases, superstition has been adapted from earlier tales. Making the sign of the cross has been replaced by giving the thumbs up.

Superstition was at its height in the 17th century. Life was insecure and escaping from poverty was at the center of human existence. Many people were farmers and dependent on the caprices of the climate. Famine, and the plague, took their toll. Life expectancy did not exceed 30 years.

All this misery needed an explanation. The cause of poor harvests and sickness were sought in the supernatural. Religion was more important than medicine. In the 17th century, superstition was almost an epidemic. Not only the lower but the upper classes also were involved with it. Witchcraft, sorcery, and many rituals, originate in the 17t century. Many tales about farming and fishery stem from those times.

Every tale has its background

The majority of the tales are based on religious legends. A Christian tale was often superstition for heathens and vice versa. During the evolution of the Western world, from the earliest heathen times until the discovery of America, religion and its impressive rituals gave rise to superstition. It explains the meaning of the mistletoe and the reason why you should not boast about your luck never to have had a rainy day on your vacation.

Mistletoe, the parasitic shrub *Viscum album* with its leathery evergreen leaves and waxy white berries, was the holy plant of the druids. When it is used as a Christmas decoration, boys can invite girls to kiss them under the mistletoe. This shrub apparently boosts women's fertility. When a boy plucks a piece of the mistletoe and gives it to the girl, the girl can retire to her room, lock the door, and swallow the berry. She scratches the initials of the boy on the leaf and sews it in her clothes, near to her heart. As long as the leaf stayed close to her heart, the boy was bonded.

Why knock on unpainted wood when you boast about never having had bad luck? One should never tempt fate. Boasting about your luck brings bad luck as sure as... fate. The origin of this superstition goes back to the Greek myths. The Greek gods always kept their eyes on the mortals' doings, and they did not like them to be too self-assured. Mortals were well advised not to draw the gods' attention to themselves too much.

Salt is one of the purest substances on earth. Therefore, spilling salt will bring fights and misfortune. That is the moment when the devil is lurking over your left shoulder. The more you spill, the nearer he comes. The solution is simple. Fling the salt over your left shoulder and give the devil the full blast. Incidentally, the salt is the first item to put in place when setting the table and the last to remove. That is why, in restaurants, the salt and the pepper is left on the table for the next guest.

Why superstition?

On our way from the cradle to the grave, we encounter many things that we cannot explain. In fact, we are part of an unfathomable mystery with incomprehensible rules. This leads to tensions and in some cases it inspires fear. Because we do not have control of everything, we lose our grip. It makes the future uncertain. Such is life that we cannot foretell the future.

With then help of superstition, we can take our future in our own hands. Superstition gives a sense of security. It is a reassurance against the uncertainty of our destiny. Unconsciously, we know that we are not following the ways of reason, but are we, humans, not as irrational as rational? Emotion oft wins from reason. When we buy a lottery ticket, we know that we are searching for a needle in a haystack. Hope however wins from the actual idea that the odds are against us.

Decreasing the uncertainty with respect to possible disaster is the basic motivation of superstition. The aim is to optimize good fortune by ruling out the uncertain dimensions of fate.

Why does everybody deal differently with superstition?

Although the basic motivation of 'ruling out the uncertain dimensions of fate' exists for everybody, everyone deals differently with this uncertainty.

We can understand and explain the different ways of dealing with superstition from two dimensions: an individual and a social dimension. We can represent them visually in a quadrant with a horizontal and a vertical axis. The individual dimension – the vertical axis – represents how one deals with the tension-regulating effect of superstition.

At the one side obtaining good fortune dominates. One wants to make the most of this good fortune. Superstition is a possibility of increasing one's good fortune and benefit from it. One sees the positive side of superstition first. The negative side, the possibility of bad luck, is more or less ruled out, rejected, or negated. This negative aspect plays the least important role in those people's lives. One can be above it or even keep the higher forces under control.

At the other side of the axis bad luck dominates. Fate is indefinable and leads to tensions. People at this side of the axis are afraid that misfortune will dominate them too much and that they themselves will lose control of their fate. Bad luck influences their lives, exercises control. They are inferior to higher powers. They feel threatened and unsure. They do not count too much on good luck. Bad luck should be averted and overcome. This leads to controlled dealing with bad luck.

The second dimension, the social dimension – the horizontal axis – refers to the communicative value of superstition, in the way in which one applies its basic meaning in the external world.

At the one side, we have the people that are attached to superstition. They believe in its consequences and recognize its advantages and drawbacks. They are led by superstition and by what their environment knows and tells them about it. In fact, you do not control superstition. Fate governs your life. Because superstition has its influence, this group adapts its behavior in order to make life as harmonious as possible. They believe superstition decreases the influence of fate. These people communicate to their surroundings that they are sensitive to superstition. By this, they let their surroundings know that this engages them in a well-considered way.

At the other side, we find strong disbelief. These people do not want to let superstition influence their lives and therefore deny its existence. Their lives should suffer the least possible negative effects because of superstition. When negative effects nonetheless do occur, they will try to find another explanation. This group will communicate about the subject of superstition in an active or a passive way.

We can distinguish four motivational needs groups in the frame of reference, i.e.

— Disbelievers,
— Fortune Hunters,
— Misfortune Avoiders, and
— Superior Beings.

Each of these groups deals with superstition in their own way.

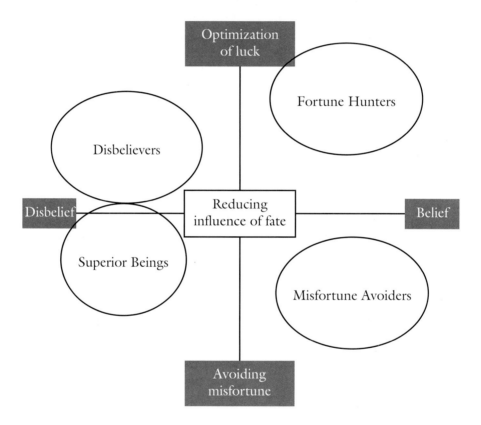

Disbelievers

The Disbelievers are found at the upper left side of the frame of reference of needs. They combine a disbelieving attitude towards the influence of fate with a positive outlook on life. The possible influence of superstition is dominated by happiness. When Disbelievers are confronted with misfortune, they will give an explanation that has nothing to do with fate.

Perception

Disbelievers have a free and open-minded attitude towards superstition. Generally, they do not even know what superstition is. They are unaware of the connotation of superstitious behavior. Disbelievers are inclined to think that one must take all one can get out of life. One is not dependent on fate; one has life in one's own hands.

"Well, let it be. If anyone thinks it's okay, he has every right to think so, but I myself don't bother with it."

The Disbelievers' attitude towards superstition is based on skepticism. They do not attach any importance to superstition and, conversely, adopt a no-nonsense attitude. They are not acquainted with the background of particular tales and do not want to know the last details. In fact, they deny the phenomenon. As they find superstition unimportant and think that it has no influence on their lives, they disregard it. Provided they know something about it, they know the positive tales; they could not care less about the negative tales.

"This is utter nonsense."
"This is something from the Middle Ages. They may have had use for it in those times, but you don't find it anymore today!"

Behavior

When it comes to superstition, Disbelievers go their own sweet way. They do not want their lives to be led by others. They do not want to be dependent on certain times, certain places and so forth. They do not want to adapt or consider it.

"I know that there is no harm in it but on the other hand I don't see the good of it. When I do not feel like it, I just think, forget it."

The Disbelievers' behavior concerning superstition is indifference, denial, or laughing it away. They turn a deaf ear to particular tales. Still, they respect the value of others. Everyone who can profit from superstition is welcome to it. Their behavior has its origin in disbelief. When you insist to know their view, they will make a joke of it. Sometimes, against their better judgment, they will not take precautionary measures; in their eyes, the immediate profit is lacking.

"On Friday 13, I really don't even think it is an unlucky day. If something goes wrong, I just think such things happen – any day. When I happen to have bad luck on Friday 13, I just treat it as a joke."

"I never read my horoscope. I don't think it's worth the time."

"Every so often I knock on wood. I've always done it. But I'm not strict about it. If I don't find unpainted wood, plastic will do."

If ever they perform a – rather elementary – superstitious act, it is because of routine. It should not become too difficult or cost too much time. They are often unconscious of the fact that those actions are based on superstition. If they knew, they would probably stop doing it.

"Putting a ring on my wife's hand when we marry, does it have a superstitious meaning? I didn't know that. Well, I think I'll rather give her a beautiful chain; everybody gives a ring anyhow."

Disbelievers do not believe in cause and effect. They will not count sheep when they cannot go to sleep. They do not see the connection between breaking a mirror and having a spell of bad luck afterwards. They think it would have happened anyway.

Fortune Hunters

Fortune Hunters, just like Disbelievers, put the positive side of superstition first. For them, good luck prevails over bad luck. With this group however superstition has a distinct place. Fortune Hunters attach importance to superstition. They want to enjoy their lives but on the basis of acceptance of what there is. By adopting this attitude, Fortune Hunters sit in the upper right side of the motivational frame of reference.

Perception

At the basis of the Fortune Hunters' perception lies the acceptance that something must be there. Superstition is a fact. It belongs there, for the whole of our lives. Fortune Hunters take it for granted that superstition is based on old folk tales. The past has established that superstition has its influence. Part of this group is indeed convinced that they have experienced the influence of superstition personally. By this acceptance, Fortune Hunters believe that they can make a balance between themselves, superstition, and their physical and social surroundings. Superstition is interwoven with everyday life.

"There are numerous old folk tales. They must surely be based on something. Since ages people are taking superstition into consideration, and for good reason."

Their attitude is positive. They take the view that you can influence good fortune by taking your surroundings into consideration, even if only little things are concerned. Optimizing good luck comes before averting bad luck. If you have done everything to avert bad luck and failed, you take it with a grain of salt. Life is not influenced by the negative things; their outlook is too positive for that.

Youri Mulder, "Good soccer players always get daughters."

We should notice two things in their attitude towards superstition. First, the hope and desire that show from their attitude. If you wish things strongly enough, in the end it will bear its fruits. Secondly, their deep interest in superstition is characteristic. This group is interested in the deeper meaning of the tales.

"My daughter is 19 but for her birthday there is still always a cake with candles she has to blow out and she can make a wish for the following year. I think it is a beautiful custom which should be maintained."

"I love to hear those stories. Why somebody holds on to a rabbit's foot for example. That's something I find interesting."

Behavior

Fortune Hunters take care of what they do in their lives; they are always willing to adapt their behavior in order to increase their fortune. They interweave superstition with their lives and their surroundings and try to influence their luck. Their behavior shows the hopes they have with respect to superstition.

Fortune Hunters do not mind taking superstition into account. When it takes time to dodge a black cat for example. They expertly execute their preventive measures. Fortune Hunters know numerous household remedies: tea with honey against a cold, warm milk when you cannot sleep, a cat on your forehead against a headache, a rusty nail under your bed against rheumatoid arthritis, an onion under your pillow against the flu et cetera. For Fortune Hunters superstition is a means one should use as much as possible. It is a help to make life more comfortable.

"Since years, I have been wearing a pair of my wife's underpants when I play an important tennis tournament. I'm sure that it brings me luck. Thanks to my wife, I've won many matches!"

Fortune Hunters link cause and effect. When they pluck a four-leaf clover and find a good friend at the door when they come home, they can link the two occurrences. They are not afraid of the negative consequences, of bad luck; they will however do everything to avoid it. Still and all, if they have the idea that they could not do more, they do not insist.

"I went to see a fortuneteller a friend of mine recommended. Well, in fact it was not a soothsayer, you know. That sounds like a fairground attraction. However, what she said was awesome. She could tell what my father looked like and how I did in school. And then she told me that I'd find true love. I'm really curious how that will turn out."

Fortune Hunters talk very openly about superstition with their family and friends. Their entourage should be convinced that it is important to allow for superstition, that superstition is important for their good fortunes. In addition to that, Fortune Hunters listen carefully to the tales. They are well informed and like to exchange good tips with acquaintances. It gives them the feeling that they help others to be happy, too.

Misfortune Avoiders

Since the Misfortune Avoiders attach great importance to superstition: uncertainty dominates their behavior. They are afraid of becoming the victims of small and greater disasters. Misfortune Avoiders are found in the lower right side of the quadrant.

Perception

This group is convinced that there are things in this world one cannot properly explain. In this, the negative dimension of adversity dominates. Misfortune Avoiders are insecure and have a feeling that imminent disaster hangs over their heads. As human beings, as individuals, they feel inferior –

and even insignificant – to higher powers around them: they constitute a threat.

Misfortune Avoiders find it difficult to accept superstition. The fear of evil or of an accident influences our lives so badly that it takes control. In fact, one's life is taken over by it. You are no longer in control of your life. Illusory threats are playing tricks on you.

"It's scary. You simply feel that it is there. I know for sure that there are higher powers."

"There are a lot of things you simply can't control. We are but a speck in the universe after all."

Emotionally, Misfortune Avoiders are weak. When they look at their surroundings, other people seem to have much more luck. Misfortune Avoiders feel that they are more often affected than others. That is how they differ from the other groups. They resent it, since they want to be like the rest. They want to belong, just like any other people; they do not want to set themselves apart. In fact, they want to be accepted by their entourage.

"It's always me!"

"You'll see. The ticket collector will always come when I forgot to punch my ticket. It cannot fail."

"I'm always the schlimazel."

In this group too, we will find many sports people, gamblers, and actors. In this case, it is all about top performances and the uncertainty of being able to pull it off. The uncertainty is great and, at that precise moment, chances are slim.

Behavior

Misfortune Avoiders have an attitude of control with respect to superstition. Fear and a feeling of menace inspire their attitude. They are unsure in this attitude; they do not know how to deal with superstition. Anyway, they find that you had better allow for superstition or otherwise things could end in disaster.

This group feels victimized. They feel powerless. They need superstition to counter it. They make sure the consequences are as bearable as possible. The only thing they can do is to execute the necessary acts as strictly as possible. Their behavior could thus be called extreme. Misfortune Avoiders will do exactly what they are taught to do and what they think is right. Only when doing strictly what is expected of them, they can avert bad luck. Superstition cannot be controlled unless you do it by the book. Thus, Misfortune Avoiders will carry out certain acts with conviction.

"Wicca – a pagan nature religion having its roots in pre-Christian Western Europe and undergoing a 20th-century revival, especially in the United States and Great Britain – has enriched my life. I think it gave me more self-assurance because I feel at home with them."

"When the moon is waxing, I don't go to the hairdresser. I go when the moon wanes, and powers wane. It's just like pruning. That too I will do when the moon wanes and I will sow while the moon is waxing."

In fact, we can point here to two different strategic behavior patterns to gain acceptance.

First, there is a group that incessantly will tell you how badly they are always being struck by misfortune. They will also tell that they do everything to avoid it. As others can empathize with them, they get a feeling that they are being accepted.

"Bad luck hangs in the air and then things begin to happen. You can't stop it. First you fail an exam, then everything goes wrong at work and then you have a row with your girlfriend to finish with."

The second group suffers in silence. They do not want to be bad style; they do not want to be different from the others. Therefore they avoid contact or keep their contacts superficial. The superstitious behavior of this group goes from bad to worse. Their behavior becomes obsessive. They often do not know themselves how badly they are doing. Because they do not want the others to be informed, they will conceal their behavior.

"When I have done it wrong, I'm sitting there the whole day, waiting for the consequences."

"I don't want others to see me in a different light just because I'm seriously involved in these things."

SIGRID JANSEN

"I do not tell my colleagues that I went to a full moon celebration. Not that I am ashamed of it but somehow it labels me. I'd have too much explaining to do."

Superior Beings

The fourth and last group, the Superior Beings, is skeptical about superstition. In fact, they do not believe in it. However, since they deem superstition negative, superstition actually plays a role in their lives. Even if you do not believe in it, you should perhaps rather be safe than sorry. Through the combination of putting bad luck at the center, added to disbelief, the Superior Beings are located at the lower left side of the frame.

Perception

In fact, Superior Beings do not believe in superstition. At least, they find it difficult to accept. They have been through so many things in life that they know they themselves have to shape their lives.

Still, they feel anxious and insecure. They feel as if they are being pestered. You can never be sure why bad luck befalls you. Superior Beings want to keep everything under control. They want to be above superstition but think they will never succeed. This feeling of incompleteness makes the Superior Beings feel inferior. They will never be in a position to bend the higher powers to their will, much as they would like to do that. As a matter of fact, being a Superior Being is more aspirational.

The fear, the uncertainty, and the feeling of inadequacy call up a sort of anger. The uncertainty about the idea that they are not their own masters makes them react against superstition.

Behavior

In order to reduce their uncertainty, Superior Beings indeed allow for superstition, just to make sure, because "there is no harm in it". Yet, they perform superstitious acts reluctantly.

"One doesn't know if it helps but I just cross myself anyway."

They also look for alternative ways to dominate their uncertainty. They invent their own rules. By developing their own initiatives, they have the feeling of being able in some way to influence the elusive powers of superstition: a degree of independence that allows them to decide what is best for them. Taking hold of the helm, they have the feeling that in some way they put themselves just a little above the 'higher powers.'

"I decide myself what I do when I spill salt. Anything you do will help ward off bad luck."

The Superior Beings however will in no way let others see that they put superstition into practice. They react against it and deal with it in a guarded way. They want to demonstrate that superstition is not founded on reality. Towards their entourage, Superior Beings behave like a sort of provocative rebels. They shift their feeling of injustice to the objective world. They will tell people who indulge in superstition that they are making fools of themselves and stubbornly deny their uncertainty.

"I have a friend and he doesn't play cards when there is cheese on the table. It brings bad luck, he says. He must be nuts!"

An example...

By way of illustration of the four groups, we can describe the behavior of the Disbelievers, the Fortune Hunters, the Misfortune Avoiders, and the Superior Beings by means of an example.

One of the best known superstitious tales is the fear of ladders. Almost everybody knows that walking under a ladder may bring bad luck. The origin of this belief goes back to Ancient Egypt where the ladder was a sacred symbol. The deceased ascended to heaven on a ladder whereas the gods descended it to earth. You can however combine good luck with walking under a ladder: just cross yourself or cross your fingers and at the same time make a wish.

Disbelievers do not take this tale for granted. They are completely indifferent to it. If the shortest way happens to be under the ladder, they do not mind. They are simply not concerned.

"What ladder?"

The Fortune Hunters however will walk around the ladder. Better be sure than sorry. Fortune Hunters are always willing to make a special effort to make sure. Their aim indeed is to be in harmony with their environment. An extra portion of good luck can always help to achieve that.

"Frankly, I do not care avoiding that ladder. After all, I took that tale in with my mother's milk."

Misfortune Avoiders will avoid ladders like grim death. On no account, they will walk under a ladder. They avoid all kinds of things that could bring bad luck: they have already had their fair share of it.

"When you walk under a ladder you're simply asking for it. Just wait and see."

When they are alone, Superior Beings will prefer to walk around the ladder. In the company of others, they take a provocative attitude: they will deliberately walk under the ladder and make a comment, too, just because they are aware of the connotations of walking under a ladder. At the same time, they feel a little uneasy but do not show it.

"Bad luck when you walk under a ladder? That's rubbish. I'm not going to make a detour for that!"

Superstition in the year now

To what extent does superstition play a part in contemporary life? Is superstition a fad? Will superstition disappear in the future or will it boom? In order to answer this question, the arguments of Prof. Helmut Gaus of the University of Ghent are workable hypotheses.

Prof. Gaus sees cyclic developments in the history of Western society. He puts that various social phenomena depend on the collective levels of anxiety and uncertainty in our society. A cycle covers a period of about 50 years: 25 years in which the level of anxiety increases whereas in the following 25 years the level of anxiety decreases. The behavior of large groups is in one way or another in a downward phase of the wave, Professor Gaus says. In a downward phase, in which uncertainty increases, anxiety, and fear can be averted, compensated, suppressed or conversely expressed by this behavior. It is a sort of biorhythm of social evolution.

Helmut Gaus describes different forms of behavior that function as alleviation of uncertainty. His research is based on extensive numerical data in which he found significant differences in the course of time. He describes for example how at the top of the wave women's fashion shows an abundance of yellow, red and orange colors. Women's liberation reigns supreme at the top of the wave. This too can be seen in fashion: feminine forms are not represented by accentuation of the waist or low necks. In times of certainty, women do not need to show their femininity; they are confident of their inner capabilities.

At the lower point, gray and black set the tone. The traditional family and the significance of marriage increase. Racism and a greater number of suicides sadly characterize the low points.

The most recent low points occurred at the end of the 19th century and just before the middle of the 20th century. Peaks occurred in the Twenties – the Roaring Twenties – and the – feminist – Seventies. Just now, at the eve of the 21st century, we are at a low. The transition to a new millennium inspires uncertainty. After the turn of the century, we have the prospect of a period of increasing certainty.

Superstition too is a form of collective uncertainty. Prof. Helmut Gaus links the expansion of magical/mythical beliefs – among which superstition – with the descending phase of the wave. During a period of uncertainty, in which one does not own much – or thinks not to own much – there is the hope that chance will bear a helping hand. In such a downward phase, one makes more ample place for luck.

Helmut Gaus says that until recently there was room for magical/mythical ways of thinking in human history; now, rationality has recovered much of the terrain. Fiction occupies a minor place. The established Churches also have lost favor.

During the last decades, the descending phase was very perceptible indeed. There was a growing interest in spirituality, all forms of meditation and games of chance. The interest in more intensive forms of belief, such as the charismatic movement, has increased. Non-denominational forms of belief, too, were – and still are – on the way up. Helmut Gaus mentions the huge successes of American televangelists and the flowering of sects. It appears even that the Virgin Mary has increased the number of Her apparitions.

In conclusion

In this paper, I have described superstition as a view of life which allows to influence one's own life by performing – or avoiding – certain acts. This vision is based on the idea that there is "more in Heaven and on Earth" than we can explain. Next to the rational, an important role has been reserved for the emotional part in human behavior. Perhaps we are letting our feelings rule us more than our intelligence. Although each person deals differently with superstition, everybody has his superstitious streak.

As a child, **Gunilla De Graef** *has always dreamed of standing on the equator one day. Her dream came true when she was eighteen. In Ecuador, where else. She has lived in Quito, 9,350 ft high in the Andes. Quito – and since then Latin America – has fascinated her.*

Gunilla, who speaks Spanish fluently, studied Latin American History at Louvain University and at the University of Barcelona, and then returned to South America in search for the New World's true character and colors.

As project leader at Censydiam, Gunilla was given even more room to test out her book learning against the reality of the continent. She has done research in Venezuela, Colombia, Peru, Brazil, in the Cono Sur countries Chile and Argentina, in the Caribbean...

It struck her that there were as many differences as similarities between the countries – or did her imagination confuse reason?

The rationale of the imagination
On market research in Latin America

Spring 1996, Belgium

(question)

My last year at university. In ex-Yugoslavia, war is drawing to and end, "until further notice." In South Africa the Truth and Reconciliation Commission has begun its work. Both countries stand on the threshold of a grand cathartic process. During a seminar on "mediation in conflicts" we present ourselves with the question: *how should and can people continue living together and working together after a traumatic episode such as a war, after terrorism, after oppression.* The process seems to be the same everywhere: drawing up political statements of principle, voting amnesty, implementing economic readjustment programs. However, what about the reconstruction of thinking, talking, planning and dreaming? Very often, little attention is paid to the human aspects of social reconstruction. *How should and can one live again on an "emotional"* basis? At the end of the seminar, more questions remain than answers have been given.

Fall 1997, Cono Sur

(hypothesis)

I am working at Censydiam since about one year. Extensive international research projects bring me through different Cono Sur countries, including Argentina and Chile. The theory of the 1996 seminar has become reality. The social reconstruction in these countries is of the order of the day; the traumatic experience of the "dirty war" has left deep marks. I become aware of it during my work here. Attempts to apply the standard projective techniques of Censydiam during in-depth interviews and group sessions bring me in direct contact with the effects of many years of social and psychological repression.

In each country, the symptoms are different.

Argentina: Borges in exile

In Argentina, the question of using imagination and fantasy provokes fierce opposition, as if this appeal to the powers of the "irrational" were a personal threat. I am aghast. What I knew about Argentina up to then were the writings of Borges and Cortázar; hard to find something more imaginative! Now this: *this sharp rationality, this heavy down-to-earthiness*, this almost physical aversion when one is asked to give one's mental nerve free rein.

Oddly enough, I do not only find this radical expressive "austerity" with adults; children too give evidence of it. "Children are too precocious here," I think after another struggle with a stubborn ten-year-old. "If he liked to go to the park with his friends," I asked. "How much am I going to be paid to answer all these questions," he answered.

When I am free for lunch, I enter a bookstore. I buy a calendar of Mafalda. Her sarcastic and smart-alecky remarks will support me when I have to face one of those rainy Belgian days, I hope. I have always thought it an ingenious idea of this comic strip artist to criticize the world around him through the figure of a child. Everybody knows that truth comes out of the mouths of babes. Of course, I took it for granted that children such as Mafalda did not exist, that she was what she was, a fiction, a simple comic strip character in the form of a young child exhibiting the voice and the way of thinking of an adult. However, when in the afternoon I have to call in my whole being and ability to interest a couple of eight-year-olds for a pastel rose and loudly yellow colored world of an animated cartoon and they look at me pityingly – "Jeez, how childish, how pathetic, that foreign woman thinking that we're going to buy this" – I suddenly realize that Mafalda and her wisecracking and fiercely rationalistic little friend Libertad – what's in a name! – really exist here in Buenos Aires and that I have met them. They exist, here in Argentina, these streetwise children with their pedantic little voices. They make me laugh sometimes but sooner make me sad: they are never pleased, never cheerful, and always on the brink of bitterness.

Chile: timidity and Enlightenment

In Chile, *timidity* is the chief defense mechanism. My invitation to imagine the package of a specific product as a person is greeted – more than in any other country – with timid coughing, uneasy feet-shuffling, hands clasping mouths or scratching heads. Fantasy appears to be an almost improper frivolity, a pastime that may be secretly attractive but condemnable in public.

I am confused. Why do the inhabitants of the southernmost part of Latin America – a continent known for its expressiveness – have so much trouble accompanying me in my playful search for emotions and personal perceptions? A conversation with a Chilean psychologist provides me with the beginning of an explanation. Elena tells me about her childhood in Santiago, about those times when even the apparently so innocent Sesame Street was censored. What was wrong with Sesame Street, I ask her. The answer was: diversity. Indeed, the existence of differences and its recognition were one of the pet topics of the program: political correctness before the term existed. Among other things, the original producers took their inspiration from the fact that Chinese children played games that were different from those American children played. For the Chilean authorities "inspiration" was seen as "insubordination." *Barrio Sésamo* in an unexpurgated version prophesized a "democratic" vision that was surely not theirs.

This Elenita was forbidden to dream about a purple tree. As soon as the ting appeared on the paper, the *maestra's* red ballpoint came into action and uprooted the absurdity. "Trees are green, Elenita, not purple. If all your classmates draw green trees, why is yours purple? Purple trees are not only a travesty of reality, they are a manifestation of a rebellious character and a non-conformist character, too." Elenita thus learned that she must not even begin coloring trees with purple because there would not be an end to it except conflicts and eventually punishment and even exclusion. Is it strange then that she remained quiet when that foreign woman reminded her of that unpleasant incident with the purple tree, slyly asking her to unlock the hiding-place of her firmly sealed fantasy?

During and after the dictatorship, Chile has produced the greatly talented author Isabel Allende, the renowned moviemakers Miguel Littín and Raúl Ruiz and many others. For a number of people, the experience of repression has been a catalyst. Their expressiveness has been eased away by a need for protest. The more they were silenced the louder and more explicit sounded their voices. However, the great majority of their fellow-countrymen have come to terms with years of silencing in a quite different way. They have learned to recognize silence and vagueness as an important survival mechanism and integrated the repudiation of fantasy as a "virtue." Now it is very difficult for them to reverse that psychodynamics.

There are of course other elements to reckon with. The person in charge of the local field agency does not entirely agree with her colleague's "psychoanalytical" interpretation of the phenomenon of limited expressiveness. She tries to present a more "classical" explanation. "Many people with whom you've talked today," she says, "are not educated, they come from a so-called 'lowly' social background. They are not used to express themselves in such a 'colorful' way." Her explanation will surely be correct, in a way, but a few interviews with people from a higher social background show that the same problem exists with the more "affluent." They too hesitate when I appeal to their imagination. Just like the *porteños* – the inhabitants of Buenos Aires – they adopt a defensive attitude. They reproach me with not taking them seriously, treating them like "any other stupid South American." That, too: regional tensions. "We are Chileans," they say, "we are more European than Latin American, you should not play these little games with us, we are not your little brothers." For the rest of the interview, these members of Chile's upper class put in every effort to convince me of the Chileans' rationality. They consider rationality as the norm and emotionality as an anomaly. They also seem to consider *rationality as a primary measure of development.* Both quite Western/European principles indeed! The "siglo de las luces" clearly has done its job here: de philosophers of the Enlightenment can congratulate themselves, in Spanish translation.

End of the year 1998, Paraguay

(thesis)

The unbearable suggestibility of being

Two years in market research now, much of it in Latin America. This is my first time in Paraguay though, a land that is often forgotten. During the interviews I am confronted with an *extreme "lack of expressiveness."* I begin my interviews with the traditional announcement – to gratify the respondents' innate vanity and gain from it. "I have heard from others that the people of this country are so communicative and like to give their opinions and hence I have high hopes for this interview." I soon understand that in this country my opening statement is a complete absurdity. Paraguayans do not at all like to talk. They are not even attracted – let alone flattered – to have a view of their own and put it forward. They clam up, seem to grudge and grouch, kill all my patience with a hundred "no sé" – "I dunno." I feel like I landed in a summer camp teeming with sulky adolescents.

GUNILLA DE GRAEF

With this last statement, I surely do not want to take anything away from the importance of Paraguayan culture. They have a unique sense of music and it is the only Latin American country where the indigenous language not only survives but also is bearer of a domestic theater and literature. I learn this when I steep myself in the history of the Jesuit *misiónes* in Encarnación. However, when I come back from the ruins of this laudable initiative to the reality of the interview room in Asunción, I am again confronted with the fact: they do not open up. I feel frustrated by the fact that it is so difficult for these people to make choices, to give an opinion, to put their personal feelings into words. Whenever I ask them about their own experience with a specific product and appraise it, they look at me distrustfully and insecurely, as if I intended to catch them in a trap, as if I was about to jump up and beat an imaginary gong: "Wrong answer, you're out."

For many years no decisions had to be taken, for many years there were no alternatives, no options, and no choices. Now, everything had to be decided: where to live, what clothes to wear, what car to drive and what beer to drink with your colleagues after work. No wonder that people found themselves in a sort of adolescent confusion. They experiment, they search, they try, and they flirt with choices but do not make any. The result is a landscape filled with billboards praising brands that since long have ceased to exist, hopelessly abandoned and fully equipped luxury apartment blocks where nobody wants to live anymore, weed-choked recreation areas, and so on and so forth. These are the monuments of a country that is ruled by hype and that of the shortest possible sort: today you are in, tomorrow you are out. In desperation, I continue to ask my respondents why they have chosen this or that brand. I know the answer beforehand. They do not know, or rather, "My uncle Carlos knew this guy who had a friend who'd heard that it was a good brand." If I saw the same respondent again the day after, he would certainly have become an ardent follower of a completely different brand and, without batting an eyelid, tell me that this was it, "because his nephew Jorge knew it from a fellow student who was now at university in the States and had seen it there on TV." Oh, the immeasurable lightness of suggestible being!

The hypothesis is itching again: difficulty to express one's opinions in a country that for years has been subjected to oppression. Ciudad del Este may have lost President Stroessner's name, a change of name does obviously not erase the past.

Detection of motivations, personal perceptions and the controlling and decision-making strategies resulting from it, that is what the Censydiam model is about. Yet, when you are confronted with *a culture in which personal motivations have been flattened down and uniformed for years*, what then?

A colleague of mine told me that my stories about Paraguay made her think of the situation in the countries of the former Eastern bloc. No doubt parallels can be drawn everywhere. Many aspects of the Censydiam model are based on the assumption of a situation of plenty, an environment in which choices have to be made, an explicitly Western situation. Yet, when fieldworkers travel farther and more deeply, they are more and more frequently confronted with other "basic elements," with *situations of scarcity* or of emerging affluence. You can call them countries in transition, or "adolescent" countries, or developing countries, the fact is that they are very critical of our ways of seeing, thinking and analyzing and that we will have to allow for it.

Spring 1999, Colombia

(antithesis)

The poetry of the diversity

While I am writing this paper, I suddenly hear a discreet ping and a small envelope flashes in the corner of my computer screen, "You have got mail." The message comes from Colombia, from my colleague and good friend Cristina. "Message" is not the appropriate word; it does no justice to the poetic prose in which Cristina – and with her most of my other Colombian friends – make even the most banal things known to the world. And while reading the text, I think: there you are, this is the antithesis. Colombia too has it fair share of terror, maybe more than any other country. Colombia too suffers war, a bitter war that gets increasingly fierce and affects every Colombian. Colombia too is full of traumas, enormous traumas that are followed every day by new ordeals. Yet, *Gabriel García Márquez is not the only one who writes beautiful words in Colombia and raises fantasy to a norm.* Cristina too, and her colleague Andrea, and her husband Jaime, and his friend Alberto are doing so. I have been listening to their anecdotes which are all of them entitled to their own place in the library of Magic Realism. And while listening to them, I think about the terrorism that has not succeeded – not yet – in crushing Colombia's imagination.

When exploring the local Colombian markets, too, I cannot but conclude that in Colombia, in spite of deadly terrorism, fantasy and creativity are still alive. Here in Colombia, the projective techniques of Censydiam do more than well: ice cream boxes are being brought into being, beer bottles are being clothed, Martians have a more than an average interest in cigarettes... Colombians have no qualms with it. On the other hand, they have their own problems. Blindfolds are better left home – kidnappings are the number one national industry. Likewise, they do not like to talk about their income – those who earn good money are *sequestrable*, "kidnappable." Still, in general, one can say that the powers of imagination and "eloquence" of the Colombian respondents makes the work of a market researcher particularly colorful and pleasant. What makes Colombia so different?

First, one could say that the Colombian situation is different from the Argentinean or Chilean situation because *in the case of the Colombians the violence is not really "institutional," it is – sad to say – "democratic."* The war that is waged in Colombia is a civil war, a conflict that is characterized by the dynamics of divergence rather than repression. Part of the civilian population took up arms against the authorities, revolted because they did not agree with the current policy. A polemic was engaged in which everybody became involved. Some joined the guerrilla, others actively engaged in getting a peace process going. Eventually, it seems that *in Colombia the pressure does not so much or only come from above but from all sides.* That makes the absolute pressure heavier but at the same time, in a certain sense, relatively lighter. Anyway, the choice of a divergent opinion – or the challenge to form such an opinion – remains a possibility.

Dictatorship does not allow contradiction. No doubt, censorship by the authorities such as it is exercised in the Cono Sur also exists in Colombia, although it is less systematic and less universal. Censorship in Colombia appears to be experienced as less stifling. Colombia tries to uphold an appearance of democracy. Dissident voices can still be heard. The budding rap movement among the youngsters in the slum areas of Bogotá is an example. The motivation among the newly graduated psychologists from the upper middle class not to gain their first work experience in expensive private clinics but as part of a scheme for AIDS patients or alcoholics can be seen as a further manifestation of divergence – maybe a less ostentatious but surely no less valuable form of social protest.

A conflict pushed along by "divergence" is how one could describe the Colombian war. In fact, "divergence" is the essence of the country. Colombia, just like Brazil, is a society that is not built on similarities but more so on differences. The exuberant geographical, botanical but also political and economic landscape is the natural soil for "divergence" and at the same time for the imagination. We could even say that censorship is not possible in Colombia because the nature of the country does not allow it.

Anyhow, upon inquiry it appears that Sesame Street at least is left in peace here. Here, trees may be purple or green or multicolored, whatever color the child wants to choose. Teaching children diversity and creativity is a virtue, not a sin, or an act of rebellion. Incidentally, that is not only due to the natural Colombian exuberance; it is related to another trait of the Colombian character: their *fondness of children*.

This is not the sort of reality-denying saying we are used to hear from do-gooders. It must be said that Colombia is indeed filled with harrowing images of street children and glue-sniffing shoeshine boys. It is the land of children adrift, of children who, together with their families, flee the impossible situations in the country, the land of hungry and abandoned children. This is harsh reality or, at least, one of the realities. In Colombia, as in all other Latin American countries, contrast and contradiction are the strongest dynamics of society. Hence I do not mind saying that apart from being the country with the greatest child misery, Colombia is also the country that has touched me most by its love of children.

In Colombia, children are indeed seen as a symbol of hope, of innocence and of freedom from care. Children are small, still untarnished spots in a country that that is weighed down with extreme and incomprehensible violence. Much attention is paid to the children's development, not only in the spheres of health care and education but also emotionally. This is what strikes me when I read the Colombian papers or watch TV. There is such a thing as a constant appeal to give room to the children's creativity.

With the children that I do interview myself, I notice their duality. Sometimes they are quite serious, and seem very much adult, when they talk about the impossibility to play in the street for example or when they are told that they cannot even go to the shop on the street corner. Then again, they are playful, light-hearted, and full of bright and colorful ideas when, for example, I ask them to invent the ideal popsicle and make a drawing of it. Magnificent constructions, rainbows of flavors, colors and designs!

This duality of the children reflects that of the whole country. Colombian children know the reality in which they live, they see the violence on television, and hear it over the radio. Sometimes you see that they do no longer know where to draw the boundary between fiction and reality. "The guy in the green uniform and the rifle, is he a soldier, a *guerrillero* or GI Joe?" Yet, they continue dreaming, drawing, and fantasizing.

Next to the character of violence and the natural diversity and exuberance of Colombia, something else can explain the Colombians' expressiveness. For many Colombians *eloquence seems to be a continuation of a fundamental national virtue: hospitality.* Colombians will not only answer any question; they will try to do it in the most entertaining way. It reminds you of the Japanese: not answering means failing in your duty towards your guest and failing in your duty towards your guest means suffering a loss of face.

This seems to be a symptom of the typical Latin American propensity for "*deber ser*," a sort of subservient pleasing behavior many Latin Americans suffer from – not taking into account the *porteños* and the inhabitants of Santiago's better neighborhoods. "*Deber ser*" literally means, "being obliged to be" and refers to the pressure to comply with the generally accepted "higher" norm.

A certain feeling of collective inferiority or victimization – the "violated" and "lost" continent – goes hand in hand here with the typical social pressure of – Latin – Catholicism. Everything is rigidly established: how a good mother ought to behave, how a woman ought to behave towards her husband, how children ought to behave towards their parents, even how a laborer ought to speak to his foreman.

During the interviews and the group sessions, the existing dynamics is again reinforced by the fact that I, the moderator of the conversations, am a European and even worse, a European woman. The response is extreme "obligingness," completely different from that in Chile, where my European origin rather caused resentment and defensive manners.

In Colombia, the feeling of collective "inferiority" seems stronger. "We are but unassuming citizens of what is a unimportant developing country," some do say, literally. People make every effort to be in my good books. As "insignificant Colombians" they thank me at great length for being able to tell their story to an ambassador of Western commercial powers. I tell them a hundred times that I do not work for the producer of the product I inquire into but the problem remains.

In Colombia, this sense of inferiority, – rooted in history, – which exist in many parts of the continent, is intensified by the present situation. It is no secret that the country is in an extremely difficult situation. It is amazing though that *all the people seem to make themselves personally responsible for the collective image of the entire country.* Colombians know very well that their country has a bad press abroad and suffer from it. Some do even speak of an "international persecution." That is why they try to influence the – good – image an outsider should have of Colombia.

Nowhere in the world I came across so many cab drivers who had such an extensive knowledge of history and newspaper stand owners who gave me such an elaborate personal analysis of the social and economic situation of their country. I cannot comment on whether what they told me was correct or not. What impressed me were the talent and the persuasiveness with which they voiced their opinions.

Colombians do talk a lot; they like to talk. Some will say that my attempts to explain the Colombians' eloquence are much too gentle and much too poetic. There has been a time indeed, when I first traveled to Colombia, that I was less than happy with the cascade of words shed onto me as soon as I crossed the border. In the beginning, I experienced the Colombian eloquence as a sort of "aggression," as a threat. I first thought that it was due to my then still limited knowledge of the Spanish language: the first time I traveled to Colombia was when – as an eighteen-year-old – I stayed in Ecuador for almost a year. In fact, I was just learning Spanish and had to ask "un poco más despacio, por favor" very often.

The melodious Ecuadorian was not much of a problem. The smooth rattling and juggling with words of the people in the occasionally hallucinating city of Tumaco on the Colombian Pacific Coast was not at all easy though. It even put me off. Native speakers however later told me that they themselves sometimes were somewhat "dumbfounded" after a conversation with a Colombian.

The "quality" of the language was surely not involved: it is common knowledge that the Colombian pronunciation is among the best and the purest of the Spanish-speaking world. It is not the velocity either: in Madrid, they are even more voluble. It must be the spontaneous "complexity" of the discourse. I can perhaps best explain it with an example of garden-variety anthropology. It is for good reason that the Colombians are considered the best salespeople of the South American continent. Whereas the
Argentinean merchant relies on slyness, the Colombian banks on his tongue; talking someone into buying something is an art that is practiced to perfection in Colombia.

Aggression, veiled feelings of inferiority or plain hospitality – for any reason whatsoever – the effect is the same: Colombians will do everything possible to be heard; an anecdote from our research practice may illustrate it.

In Colombia, we always invite a number of reserve candidates for the group sessions, not only to make sure of having sufficient participants but also to be able to choose those who correspond best to our criteria.

One evening, twelve people were waiting to form a group that eventually would comprise only six. When the screeners had finally been filled out and the "chosen few" had entered the room where the group session had to take place, the others who remained behind looked rather beaten. The receptionist who had welcomed the group pointed this silent grief out to me. I too thought it a shame they had wasted their time and said, "They get their reserve compensation, don't they? In Belgium, people would be glad to receive money and having nothing to do to earn it." The receptionist answered, "Yes, that may be true in Belgium but this is Colombia. Those people consider it a duty and also an honor to talk with you. They take your invitation to talk with you very seriously. They can't get in now and think they have not come up to the mark. They think that there is something wrong with them." I was standing there, biting my nails. I am the last to look down on someone's commitment. So we decided that – to smooth ruffled feathers – one of my colleagues of the local field agency would do a "rescue interview" with the respondents who were to be left behind. I saw them walk into another room, relieved: they would be able to tell their story after all.

A few hours later all groups had finished. When everything was cleared up, the colleague who had monitored the reserve group came to me. She had quite a few small cards in her hand. It appeared that a number of respondents in the "mock-up group" had left their names and addresses "in case the Belgian lady would have more questions to ask after all." Q.E.D.

Summer 1999, back in Belgium

(answer?)

Hypothesis, thesis or antithesis? After months of hectic round trips between Belgium and Latin America, I decide to stick to the first, for the time being. I have not yet found a conclusive and sound answer to my question. It does not really matter though. Even if it remains a hypothesis, it is still very captivating. The war in former Yugoslavia which almost ended in 1996 flared up again and, according to some, precisely because the "healing process" in the human sphere had been ignored. South Africa is building a new future but without a great part of its former inhabitants; many chose to leave the country, possibly because for them personally the healing process did not pass off as they had hoped or expected. The arrest of Augusto Pinochet in London revealed that in Chile the healing process is much farther away than the economic development of the Latin American tiger did hold up: the impossibility to talk openly of healing the dictatorial trauma again opposes the people into two sharply divided camps, and so on and so forth.

How people do reconstruct not only their country, their economy, and their society after a traumatic period, but also how it affects their personality, their "deeper" being, remains a crucial question on a global level. For us, cross-cultural and international researchers, this is a "vital" question. The ability to express oneself, the powers of imagination, and the capacity to make one's own choices and form one's own opinions are the main objects of our research. How wars, terror, or even "latent" conflicts are influencing these, concerns all of us.

Henk Eising *(1955) studied both the teaching and the research branches of Social Geography at the University of Amsterdam. He graduated in urban city issues and, specifically, the process of gentrification, a subject on which he has published various papers. After his studies, research proved to be more appealing than teaching and he joined Motivaction Amsterdam, where he held different positions as researcher.*

In 1990, Henk Eising made the changeover to private enterprise and accepted the position of market researcher at Heineken Netherlands. In 1996, he was appointed Market Research Manager at the Corporate Marketing Department and became responsible for research in the Caribbean and in Latin America.

Sport – in the broadest sense – is Henk's passion. He is a keen soccer player, cyclist, tennis player and skier, though the time to practice those is rather limited – especially when two daughters, too, call for attention. Writing short stories and columns is another of his interests of which the following tale gives evidence. It recounts in an amusing way that fieldwork can sometimes interfere with field... sports.

Sorrow on the field and... in the field

The eve before my departure to Venezuela was one I'll not likely forget. The summer had set in yet – although considerably late – and brought the thrill announcing the arrival of something sensational to the city of Amsterdam. Everywhere around us, people – rigged out in the oddest ways as long as it happened to include the color orange – were on their way to cafés or to friends. The World Cup soccer competition in France was in full swing and the great day of the quarterfinals had come. The Netherlands against Argentina. If that wasn't going to be a knockout! An hour and a half later a storm filled the torrid evening air. Just before the end of the match, Dennis Bergkamp had brilliantly shot Oranje to victory. Two matches to go and the World Cup was ours! But first the semifinals. Against the Brazilian gods!

Little by little my euphoria turned to gloominess. I wouldn't see it happen: professional obligations in Venezuela! Whereas my friends normally take note of my business trips to exotic places with envy, this time they let me know that Caracas was definitely not the place to be in the next few days. I couldn't but agree with that. It very rarely happens that I regretted so much that they would stay in Amsterdam while I went abroad.

Soccer is not exactly the sport in which Venezuelans excel. They do, on the other hand, in beauty contests. In a normal course of events, that would have been a nice prospect but these days, other things were more important. My fears that the World Cup wouldn't even be transmitted in Venezuela grew hand over fist. Fancy going through this: we're about to win the World Cup and you ain't going to witness it. Except maybe for two minutes on CNN and a commentary that is not hampered by an excess of expert understanding. The very thought of it drove me nearly crazy.

Caracas is hot and humid when I land. On the plane, I couldn't leave off torturing myself with reading the jubilant commentaries of the night before and the warm-up stories about the match to come against the samba dancers. Gunilla is already there. As a skilled project leader, she has already taken quarters at the local field agency. Listening patiently to my lamentations, she manages to let me know that there is no TV set. Or rather that there is one but it is to be used for showing commercials during the group discussions. There you are! I knew it!

The day of the match arrived. Nine o'clock in the evening at Western European Daylight Time meant 3:00 PM here. Right in the middle of the group discussion! Sheer desperation began to seize me. Again, I tried to raise the matter gently with Gunilla. My Spanish not being in the same league as Gunilla's, I must have missed what she has discussed in her castellano tête-à-têtes with the director of the field agency. However, the customer is always right and that was made crystal clear to me very soon. The morning group discussion will be dispatched of double quick, after which we will go to a classy restaurant where the match will be shown on a large screen! I felt like kissing her! I did.

Talkers as they are, the Venezuelan respondents had spun out the group discussion unnecessarily long, so we rushed to be on time at the restaurant. No picnic, as I see that the roads are overcrowded with people in search of a large or as the case may be a smaller TV screen to watch the game of their heroes — which do not happen to be the Dutch. Ain't those Venezuelans interested in the World Cup?

We arrive at the restaurant just in time. The best table has been reserved for our party. The other guests are greeting me with smiles and giving me the thumbs up. It must be my orange suspenders. An exquisite choice of dishes and ice-cold Heineken's are being served. The match can begin. I'm as happy as a child.

The last penalty shot by Ronald de Boer is received with deafening shouts. He missed. Brazil goes to the final. When I shrink with disappointment, I feel consoling hands on the back of my head. The pesos I've wagered are being swiped from the table. Guests who a moment ago looked reasonably civilized now change into roaring lions. Tables collapse under loads of dancing people. A squirt of uncorked champagne douses the imposing décolletage of a handsome woman behind me. Where am I? In Rio? In São Paulo?

Outside, the sunlight hurts my eyes. The noise of thousands of cars honking is even worse. Brazilian flags and blasts of samba-house blow from a myriad of lowered car windows. My mouth hangs open in amazement. How is it possible that a city of twelve million inhabitants blows its top for the achievement of another country? Would this be possible in Europe? Well, yes, when a not too well loved neighboring country *loses*, maybe. The chief of the field agency has the answer. "We love life," he says. "That's why we are always on the lookout to celebrate something, something to rejoice at. And that need not necessarily be ourselves, quite contrary; as it does not happen to us very often, we rejoice at the good fortunes of others."

In the evening, when we try to grab a cab on our way to the hotel, we find that the Venezuelan 'Weltanschauung' is still emphatically being put into practice. "Imposible... El centro estará congestionado con fiestas populares," the taxi driver announces, which in a free translation means that we shall have to go on foot. One big singing and dancing and especially drum-beating crowd is our lot. The yellow and green of the Brazilian T-shirts and tank tops predominate. I can clearly see now why the Venezuelans always score well at beauty contests. And laughing faces everywhere, everywhere. The exuberant mood jumps over upon us and so we have another one, to Brazil. Or rather, to Venezuela.

My thoughts turn to the home front. No laughing faces there now if I remember well the gloom of earlier deceptions. With hindsight, it is not so bad to be in Caracas. My friends will envy me.

Jempi Moens *is a Fleming who heads Censydiam's "outpost" in the Netherlands. "Outpost"? Antwerp and Amersfoort lie only a two hours' leisurely drive apart! Antwerp sits all but on the border between Belgium and the Netherlands – or should we say: on the "frontier"?*

The Dutch and the Flemings; can there be two more closely linked peoples in the European Union? The Dutch and the Flemings are neighbors, they speak the same language, and yet, in some of their behavior, they are light-years apart.

The Dutch have given their name to quite a number of expressions in English – rather unfavorable expressions, alas, and quite undeservedly. Well, at least it gives the Dutch a clear-cut – though false – identity. The Flemings, on the other hand, are badly in need of an identity; an identity they lost when the Netherlands or the Low Countries – of which they formed a part – disintegrated and the southern provinces became a new country, Belgium, in which their culture withered away under the domination of the French-speaking provinces. That was a century ago. And now?

Censydiam has always given emphasis to the importance of the role feelings of inferiority and the need for self-assertion play in individual consumer behavior. As a Dutch Fleming – or a Flemish Dutchman – Jempi Moens is very well placed to observe the role those feelings play on the level of a whole people as well.

The Dutch and the Flemish
Speaking the same language, yet in different tongues

"What does a Fleming do when he goes bald? He buys hair-lotion. And a Dutchman? ... He immediately sells his comb."

"How do you drive a Dutchman crazy? Put him in a circular room and tell him he can find a guilder in a corner."

Everybody knows them, the reciprocal — and interchangeable — jokes, packed with stereotypes, that portray the Dutch as (hyper-) assertive and stingy and the Flemings as sociable yet naïve and ignorant.

Such jokes exist in all neighboring cultures. The jokes the French tell at the expense of the Swiss, the English about the Scots and so forth, are of the same caliber. I am talking about the Dutch and the Flemings here, but the mechanisms are roughly similar everywhere.

It is common knowledge that humor acts as a safety valve. It is a means of releasing tension, and making 'strangeness' the subject of a safe discussion. The jokes different cultures tell about each other invariably refer to these peculiarities and tensions.

Tensions? What tensions? We speak the same language, we live and work in each other's countries, we do good business with each other, and we read each other's literature...

Apparent similarities are obviously deceiving us. Moreover, we very often are oblivious to this deception. The uneasiness, the incomprehension, the area of tension that normally exist between two different cultures, manifests itself in a much subtler way than between very explicitly different (different language speaking) cultures.

After eight years spent in the Netherlands, Dutch people keep asking me — rather mockingly — what makes a Belgian come to the Netherlands when Belgium is such an enjoyable, exuberant — and tax-friendly — country.

The Dutch are also interested in my adaptation process. Will I stay a Belgian or will I after all adopt the Dutch nationality? At the same time my

Belgian friends want to know if it is "at all possible to get used to live in the Netherlands" and are curious to know whether I had to forgo any pleasures in — strictly Calvinistic — Holland. Did I say: intercultural uneasiness?

The business lunch ritual is another good example. The amazement of the Belgians at the sandwiches with a glass of milk or buttermilk! Then again, the amazement of the Dutch at the extensive lunch with beer or wine — just like that, during working hours.

These differences in mentality, customs, and habits did not arise suddenly and haphazardly. They have deep roots in our cultural history.

Merchants and farmers

The geographical history of the Netherlands is characterized by a permanent struggle against the assault of the sea and the drainage of polders. For centuries they had to fight, to keep their heads — literally — above water and make their soil fit to live on.

In fact, the Dutch were dependent on trading and on an extravert, expansive spirit. It is no coincidence that they play an important role in world trade and that they are the distribution center of Europe. Neither is it a coincidence that the Dutch exude their identity in such a self-confident manner.

Belgium has been an agricultural country and remained so for a very long time. Belgians had to depend on themselves — and became resourceful wheeler-dealers and artful dodgers in the process. They did not need extravert entrepreneurship, which the various occupiers the country's history has known — Spaniards, Austrians, French, and Dutch — would soon crush anyway.

Belgians are much more circumspect; they are more introverted than the Dutch and wait to see the way the cat jumps. At the same time, being accomplished compromise-producers and crafty devils, they learn how to live with a situation and make the best of it.

Less well known is the fact that in 1585, when the Spanish occupied Antwerp and secured the southern Netherlands, Flanders, and Brabant for Spain and blocked Antwerp from sea trade, the more enterprising Flemings emigrated and played an important role in the Netherlands — in the Dutch East India Company amongst others.

Calvinism and Catholicism

Strikingly few Belgians and Dutch are aware of the influence of Calvinism and Catholicism on our behavior and mentality. Of course, we are all familiar with the stereotypes — the parsimonious Dutchman and the exuberant Belgian — but very often, we do not understand the more subtle differences that manifest themselves in our daily contacts.

Belgians do not understand why the Dutch — and not only the children but the adults too — are so crazy about chocolate sprinkles. The Dutch for their part do not understand why Belgians eat a chocolate bar with their sandwich.

In the Dutch view, eating chocolate sprinkles is a clever compromise that allows them to eat chocolate in a justifiable way. Belgians consider chocolate sprinkles an infantile and worthless product.

From that same angle, we develop totally different rationalizations for the products we use. The Dutch 'health sandwich' — as they call French bread with cheese, ham, lettuce, gherkin, and eggs — is majestic overindulgence with a perfect health-rationalization, even if it is spread with butter and mayonnaise. The Belgian equivalent — which goes under the telling name of 'gunk sandwich' — is self-indulgence without any rationalization about health.

More eating habits

The Dutch eat with their heads, the Flemish with their stomachs. Reason against emotion. Too simple a representation of the facts? It has nevertheless a grain of truth in it.

The Dutch have more of a guilty conscience when it comes to the point of physical pleasure. There is the danger of excess and loss of control. The Dutch are very good at combating this sense of guilt connected with pleasure. They have devised all kinds of strategies. They rationalize their dealing with pleasurable products — "tasty but good for your health too" — they create situations in which a certain form of pleasure is permissible or make products whose use can be easily rationalized. The Dutch have developed a 'smartness relation' with food. A greasy product accompanied by a healthy salad is plainly rationalized as a sensible meal. Besides, there are strictly regulating norms such as drinking a glass of milk around noon but along with that there is a strong 'snack culture' to escape from the norm.

The — catholic — Belgians, on the other hand, know how to live with the concept of sin: when you overindulge you can always fast afterwards and there will always be a day when you will do a little bit more exercise and make up for it.

Belgians deal with feelings of guilt in a more passive way. They accept them or do something about it after the fact. Belgians do not have so many of those cleverly devised compromise products with which they can avert guilty feelings.

This lack of complication results in consuming a greater variety of products. The Dutch are utterly amazed at what they see as the Flemish immoderation such as regularly eating lobster, oysters, fillet steaks — on ordinary weekdays — and drinking champagne — on any day other than on a birthday or New Year — or using cream or wine, champagne and beer in recipes for everyday dishes.

The cultural and historical background described above still influences our behavior and actually causes many misunderstandings between the Dutch and the Flemings. Because of the fact that we think we resemble each other, we misjudge our differences.

And they are many...

Social control. The Dutch never draw the curtains of their living room.

The Dutchman's spirit of enterprise also finds its expression in his social contacts. Dutchmen are most proficient in networking. In addition, they are very tolerant to divergent opinions and behavior. In the Netherlands, it is not very difficult to make people's acquaintance: just introduce yourself and offer a drink. A quite straightforward process.

The same goes for business contacts, which makes doing business with the Dutch rather pleasant. Everyone knows were they stand, there is a well-defined agenda to go on, and there are well-defined rules and agreements.

The other side of the coin is the feeling of superficiality one gets. It is often said that the Dutch are cold and unemotional negotiators. Gifts are seen as bribery and business lunches as a waste of time.

After business too, the Dutch appear to be more superficial or at least want to keep their emotions under control. Deep emotions are not often shared with others. In everyday language a variety of emotions are reduced to a set of unspecific expressions such as 'nice', 'funny', 'pleasant'...

Social life is strictly regulated and social control is organized in community centers, pressure groups, and so forth. In the evenings, Dutch families will never close the curtains of their living rooms: everyone must be able to see — and control — what goes on there.

Business and organization culture

Roughly speaking, we can state that different principles underlie the business and organization culture in the two countries. The average Belgian business culture is orientated towards the individual and is strictly hierarchized — a Latin trait.

The Dutch culture is based on egalitarianism; its structure is less hierarchical — the Anglo-Saxon trend. People are treated according to their function — and it is on this basis that they are answerable to their bosses. Their function itself is the basis for consultations.

In Belgium, people are treated on the basis of their capabilities — or shortcomings — and their importance within the hierarchy.

The well-organized consultative culture in the Netherlands is in contrast with the authoritarian culture in Belgium. In Dutch business culture, one has to stand up for oneself — low as one may hierarchically be. In Belgium, it is more a question of making good use of one's qualities — and thus gaining importance — without disturbing the hierarchy.

In Belgium, assertiveness is not by definition a positive quality or a guarantee for success whereas it is the norm in the Netherlands.

This often has particular consequences for common consultations: the Dutch assemble a party for a meeting based on functions, Belgians because of the — presumed — importance of its members.

That goes for the agenda too. In Belgium, it is logical that the highest in the hierarchy lays down the agenda. In the Netherlands, the group decides — by deliberation, everyone contributing an item by virtue of his function.

Belgians very often find the Dutch too aggressive and too direct. But then again the Dutch find that the Belgians generally do not come to the point and are not pragmatic enough.

An important difference between the two, and a source to many misunderstandings, is the difference between the context-oriented culture of the Belgians and the job-oriented culture of the Dutch. This difference in approach and cast of mind quite often causes a breakdown in business negotiations, take-over bids, or efforts to set up an association.

Belgian business culture is oriented toward relationships. The Belgian executive sounds out the context. He wants room to get to know his prospective partner — or colleague — so that he can enter a relationship. He loves the rituals that can help him achieve this — inviting a prospective partner for drinks or for lunch, taking him around the factory and so on. The substance of the first conversation is not important; the atmosphere is. The atmosphere determines how the future association will be — if it comes into being at all.

Dutch business culture is job-oriented. A Dutchman approaches his prospective business partner or colleague in a direct way. He wants to get on with business and/or enter into an agreement as soon as possible. He recommends what is to recommend, makes clear what his expectations are, asks if there are more questions, and steers toward a decision or a future appointment. What matters is the subject of the conversation and nothing else. More often than not, he will also forward a proper report of the conversation. The atmosphere is beside the question: it does not fit with his habit of mind. It is unthinkable — within the job-oriented approach — to found the advisability of an association on 'atmosphere' or on impressions.

This difference in mentality brings with it confusing situations and misunderstandings. Imagine a discussion of progress between Belgian and Dutch colleagues. In their mentality, the Belgians will think of who should be present — who is important? Where should the meeting take place? Which is the atmosphere that suits the purpose and the scope of the meeting? Then there is the food — feeling good, showing generosity and so on. At last, the agenda. Who should have his say? How do we tackle sensitive questions and problems? How do we humor everyone?

The Dutchman's comment on such an approach will be: "It was convivial alright but, to my mind, we didn't achieve anything," or: "Drinks before noon, an extensive four-course lunch, wine with the meal... what a waste of time!" It also happens that the Dutch have questions about the presence of colleagues who, in consideration of their function, do not belong there but are, hierarchically, important for the firm.

The Dutch mentality prescribes to organize such a meeting pragmatically and efficiently. The composition of the agenda comes first. Items should be submitted a week in advance; so is the maximum time to present one's item. Tasks will be assigned: who will preside, who will moderate, who takes minutes? The locale will be within easy reach for everyone. Atmosphere and catering obviously come second: "Taking a quick bite is just as enjoyable" or "A pleasant drink at the end can be quite entertaining, too."

As things are with the Dutch, Belgians habitually complain about the lack of hospitality — and in the worst case have a feeling of not being taken seriously — or they make jokes about the parsimony and the masochism of the Dutch. The Dutch do not quite follow that: they feel that they have taken care of everything in good time, that everything has been planned with care to make it an efficient day, and yet...

Education

Our cultural differences also show in the way in which we educate our children.

In the Netherlands, education, too, expresses the collective mentality with regard to equality, authority, and self-expression. The Dutch teach their children to make independent judgements and treat others as equals. Dutch society is indeed built on those principles — freedom of speech, tolerance, and equality. Differences are tolerated and even encouraged, on condition that one can put it into the perspective of one's environment: "Just act normal, you'll look ridiculous enough," as the Dutch saying goes.

The average Belgian parent finds that Dutch education delivers children who are much too liberal and even impertinent. Belgian children are being socialized and prepared to take part in society in a clearly different way. Here, the stress is put on becoming aware not only of one's qualities but also of one's limitations, on always doing one's best, on being polite and unassuming, and respecting others — always asking for permission and approval.

Living apart together

How do you drive a Belgian crazy? Ask him to start a business in the Netherlands... No, it did not get that bad! However, it is of vital importance to appreciate the differences and the misleading similarities and most certainly the mutual misunderstandings. For the researcher too this essential.

If you are not aware of that, chances are that you keep making the same mistakes, hitting the same stumbling blocks and getting annoyed at the same differences until the end of time.

In my personal strategy to develop and feel happy — privately as well as in my professional life — a strong awareness of these circumstances has played an important role. As well as the intent to blend the best of both cultures for my family and myself.

I like the businesslike straightforwardness of the Dutch but combine it with the Belgian candor, creativity, and personal commitment. The greater social tolerance and freedom of the Dutch can also perfectly be combined with the Burgundian lifestyle of the Belgians.

In a short: as long as you are open to cultural differences and their origin, working and/or living in another culture soon becomes an enrichment for yourself — and your environment. If you coop yourself up in the principles of your own culture, it will be a perpetual source of annoyance, frustration, and incomprehension.

Mireille Berends *is a textbook example of a cross-culturally correct student. She chose to read both Economic and... Cross-cultural Psychology. Indeed, in the Netherlands, the latter branch of studies does exist. It figures in the roster of the Tilburg University.*

Mireille has chosen Cross-cultural Psychology because she has a cross-cultural history herself. As a child she has lived in the German-speaking part of Belgium and spent her teenage years in Great Britain. She has chosen Economic Psychology in view of becoming a market researcher.

Was it pure chance that she did her practicum at Censydiam for Kids? No. Mireille loves children. And marketing. The practicum consisted in mapping motherly roles. The year was 1992. A year later, one week after her graduation, Mireille became a Project Leader at Censydiam for Kids. The task took her all over Europe, exploring the worlds of computer games and candy – or tuck, as she remembered it from her years in a British school. At present, Mireille Berends is Research Director at the Dutch branch of Censydiam for Kids in Amersfoort.

Considering her background, it is not surprising that when Mireille wonders what sort of marketing is cross-culturally most correct, global or local, the answer turns out to come from the mouths of children.

Global or local marketing? Ask the children

Based on my own experience and not on theory, I would like to try to persuade the reader that global marketing is perhaps not always the best thing. In fact, it only rarely works. Needs and motivations might be the same all over the world but the ways in which they are expressed are highly dependent on the culture one lives in.

The social norms, beliefs, and traditions of nations play an important role in determining behaviour. Behaviour that seems very normal in your own country might be rejected and even provoke aggression in other countries. The first thing that comes to mind is the differences between Western religions and Islam. Most people know that you should not serve pork to a Muslim. If you did not know this, you would find yourself in a rather awkward situation.

Much closer to home even, you will find that there are many differences between the countries and even between the different regions within the same country. Experiencing the differences between Belgium and the Netherlands, which on the surface appear to have very similar cultures — neighbouring countries where the same language is spoken — makes you wonder how much countries further from home will be different. What I am really trying to say is that when global brands develop their marketing strategies they should not forget nor underestimate the local cultures they are dealing with.

Europe, different cultures and different... stereotypes

People tend to have specific impressions of different countries. When one thinks of France, the picture of a man with a moustache and a beret, garlic round his neck and a baguette under his arm comes to mind. Holland is associated with tulips, windmills, clogs, cheese, and cheese girls. A stiff upper lip, gin and tonic, double-decker busses, and the Royal Family saga are some of the typical associations with Britain.

Taking a closer look at the Dutch, they are thought to be tolerant, assertive, and direct in expressing their views, and Calvinistic. They are also said to be very parsimonious and great savers. However, despite this thrift and the tendency to save one's money, you will see the Dutch going on holiday all over the world. How do they do it?

On their journeys, they will take along with them all they can carry. Their cars are fully packed with food and other necessities from back home. Who hasn't been to Disneyland Paris and seen the Dutch queuing for a ride whilst eating biscuits ('stroopwafels') and drinking soft drinks they brought along from home? It is not surprising that the Dutch are renowned for their caravans. In the summer months, there is an exodus of caravans to the southern sun. What could be more Dutch than taking your own home with you, with everything in it that you might need on your holiday?

Is this typically Dutch? It can be said that this small country is gradually loosing its identity. Is the Netherlands not becoming a multicultural community where most things are tolerated and where one often turns a blind eye? Yet, there appears to be an upsurge in patriotism. Just look at the general interest in Dutch football, "the orange feeling," as the Dutch call it. Even McDonalds now has a Dutch burger — available in the Netherlands only — the "McKroket."

There seems to be an increasing need for a Dutch feeling, and I am sure that this need is not only present in the Netherlands. The need to belong is a very basic need and just as there is a need to belong, there is a need to be different from the others, in this case to be different from other countries and/or cultures.

With the coming of United Europe, there is still the need to be different, but it will be much more difficult to differentiate oneself within Europe. There might no longer be borders and the money will all be the same but one will still search for other ways to be different. In the worst case, I shall expect Europeans to look for differentiation outside Europe. Other continents will bring other cultures.

Pull up your socks and eat your horse steak

A few years ago, the IRA exploded a bomb in Hyde Park. It was a nasty bomb, filled with large nails. It had been placed underneath a stage on which a military band was playing. The band and many people in the crowd were confronted with a spectacle that was quite horrific. Several members of the band died; others lost limbs. Those unharmed were left with a traumatic experience. It appeared that not only people had been severely hurt, but also a horse.

The event was, not surprisingly, in the news for several days. What really struck me though, was that so much attention was given to the horse. Many people sent the horse get well cards and the media closely monitored its recovery. Except for the number of wounded and dead, nothing more was said about the human victims. The horse was all that mattered. The horse had captured the hearts of the British public.

It became clear to me that for the British, horses must be very precious, almost sacred animals. This is certainly not the case in the Netherlands. Looking at the difference in appreciation of the animal, I am not surprised that our Dutch 'frikadel' — a minced-meat hot dog you can eat in every Dutch snack bar — is not a hit in the UK, considering that it is partly made from horsemeat. I am sure you will agree with me that knowing the difference in attitude towards horses can be essential in determining marketing or communication strategies or even the introduction of related products.

Another occasion I would like to share with you because I feel it might be of interest, happened during a music lesson in the UK. I had been in the UK for about five months, three of which during the summer holidays, so my English had improved but I was certainly not fluent.

We were being taught about specific composers, and then suddenly our teacher addressed the class. I had not heard or did not quite catch the first part of her remark, but I did hear her say that we needed to pull up our socks. I thought it was a rather strange request but hearing the tone in which she said it, I quickly decided to pull my school uniform socks up, literally. My teacher became quite angry with me: "Don't think you are being funny," she said. I was not trying to be funny. She was angry with me and I could not understand why. Had I not done exactly what she asked?

Looking back on it, I think it was a rather funny situation. It made me realise that you really need to live within the cultural context to get an exact feeling of all the different meanings words can have and the ways in which word combinations can be used.

Learning a foreign language from a book or learning a foreign language at school is sufficient to carry on a simple conversation but not enough to understand the language fully. To grasp a language it is necessary to spend time in the country in question. Furthermore, one does not learn slang and colloquial language from books.

I feel that a language is carried by culture. The Dutch language has only one word for snow, namely 'snow'. It is the same with Spanish. The German language has some more. The Eskimos however have an enormous range of words to describe specific qualities of snow. For the Eskimos, snow is not just snow.

When you apply this idea to marketing, you can imagine the importance of testing communication and in fact check it locally. Just imagine using a pay-off which is completely misunderstood in one country whilst it is a great success in another country.

Eating in a posh restaurant or eating cheap or...

Here is another interesting observation, which I feel supports my feeling about global marketing. You may find Chinese restaurants all over the world. Yet, what is on the menu in each country has clearly been adapted to suit the needs and wants of each country. The first time my family and I went out for a Chinese meal in the UK, we soon discovered totally different habits. Looking at the menu, we noticed that the rice was priced separately. We found this rather strange. Not knowing whether to order it separately or not, my father ordered one serving of fried rice. It turned out to be just enough for one person.

We also found that Chinese food in the UK was more exclusive and more of a delicacy than in the Netherlands. When you have a Chinese meal in the Netherlands, rice is served with every dish. The servings are large and low-priced. The average Chinese restaurant in the Netherlands looks more like a snack bar than an exclusive restaurant.

Dealing with food appears to be influenced by culture in a large measure. No Dutch person in his right mind would think of eating baked beans, Danish pastries, or muffins for breakfast. Yet, in the UK, baked beans are an essential part of a substantial English breakfast, and breakfast in the US generally consists solely of muffins and Danish pastry. The Americans would think twice about eating a slice of bread with cheese or chocolate spread in the morning.

Eating the "right" kind of food

In France, Spain and Italy, baker's shelves are full of cakes, whilst in the Netherlands the choice is rather limited. These cakes are available in these southern countries in all shapes and sizes and also as special cakes for kids and even eaten for breakfast. In the Netherlands cake is seen as a rather adult product and generally only eaten at teatime.

In the UK, crisps are perceived to be nourishing and generally thought to be part of an everyday lunch. This is even more the case in America where crisps can even be part of a meal – in a restaurant. BLT's are often served with crisps.

In the Netherlands however, crisps are perceived to be rather unhealthy –fattening, too rich in calories, too greasy, and not nutritive enough. They are eaten mostly in the weekend, Birthdays or on a get-together. Mothers often use them as a reward and as a treat. Crisps in the Netherlands mainly have a social function, nibbling together.

Reading the above, I realised that this in fact is also a good example of the effect culture can have on a language. It appears to matter whether one reads it with an American or British background. What is meant with the word crisp is very clear for someone with British affinity. Yet American minded people (cultures with American influence) might find the use of crisps rather confusing. Using potato chips instead of crisps might clarify the above passage. I suspect that someone unfamiliar with the British culture might automatically assume that it must be French fries or chips the British eat with their sandwiches. One would probably find it hard to believe that the British and Americans actually eat potato chips/crisps with their meals.

You can imagine how my mother, who is Dutch, felt when my sister and I kept nagging her to put crisps in our lunchboxes every day, like all the other British children were having at school. To my mother, crisps meant giving her children something unhealthy and giving it at a time when healthy food is most essential. We certainly had a hard time persuading her. We ended up compromising. Once a week we were allowed to choose a packet of crisps for lunch.

The perception of crisps – their function and the moment of giving them to the children – differs from one country to another. There is nothing exceptional then in assuming that marketing this product needs to be different and in each of these countries and adapted. When you come to think of it, it is the same with ice cream. In the US and Southern Europe, ice cream has a nutritious value whilst in Northern Europe it is seen as a sweet, as an indulgence.

Adam's ale, the best brew?

The idea of belonging, the need to feel that you are part of a group, which is highly present with teenagers, is probably a need that is of importance worldwide. You are bound to find teenagers in England, in America but also in Indonesia who feel insecure and are strongly influenced by their peers.

Yet, the way in which this is expressed in behaviour will certainly differ. In American cities, you have the extreme cases of gangs who feel the need to belong to a group in order to survive on the streets, the Blues versus the Reds. Travel books advise not to wear these specific colours in certain regions of America; you might be mistaken for a member of just such a gang.

In England, drinking alcohol seems to be a very important social factor. The English have always known to be great drinkers. This goes back to the good old days of the Empire. Remember the characters from W. Somerset Maugham's short stories drinking their very civilised gin and tonic in a far-off jungle outpost. Furthermore, the rather strict alcohol legislation in Britain – you must be 18 to be served alcohol and pubs still have early closing times, which favoured the development of 'drinking clubs' — also seems to foster this obsession with alcohol.

Alcohol is a big thing with teenagers, even to the extent that it is rather cool to drink and drive. I had a hard time persuading someone who had drunk a large amount of alcohol not to get behind the wheel. To him it was the most normal thing. No surprise if you consider that his friends were showing off about not being caught for drink-driving, even after having caused an accident. You might say that you will find these teenagers in the Netherlands also, and I will agree, but the difference is that, in the Netherlands, alcohol is dealt with much more naturally. It is not as much of an obsession as for the English teenagers.

To belong or not to belong, that is the question

British children and teenagers generally have few after-school activities apart from the football club for boys. British children and teenagers practise sports mostly at school. In the Netherlands, my own experience is that teenagers mainly know each other from clubs, especially from sports clubs. Dutch children and teenagers have a busy life after school. They often belong to many different clubs and that is where in general the peer groups are formed. I also feel that the pressure of the peer group is stronger in the Netherlands.

I remember my cousins telling me about children going into shops, cutting the Lacoste crocodiles from T-shirts in order to sew them on their T-shirts so that they would not be excluded from the group. And what about the Flippo? The Flippo was a promotional article that came with Smiths crisps. It was trendy for quite a while and children would bully younger children to do them out of them or steal them from the crisps bags in the shops.

I would like to quote something a mother told me about her child: "I didn't buy Smiths crisps to start with but you should have heard my daughter. She said I didn't love her as I didn't buy the Smiths crisps for her." Everyone at school had to do so in order not to be the odd man out. You made sure to own some.

Torn between family and peer group

What I am really trying to demonstrate with these anecdotes is that I do not really believe in global marketing. There are certainly specific motivations and needs you will find across the world, but it is my firm belief that every country has its own customs, traditions, ideas, norms and values, which we should not underestimate.

In our research at Censydiam for Kids, we apply a systematic approach. We look at children and teenagers in their environment. Children and teenagers live in a social environment. First, it is the family. Later, the peer group — friends — gains in importance. There is a lot of opposition between the needs of the different members of these systems, but good marketing concepts help to overcome these oppositions. To understand the evolving needs of children, one has to understand the communication and interaction between children and their parents, and between children and their peers. Here we will solely look at the interaction between children and parents, within the family system. It appears useful to classify different types of families:

— In a mothering family, children are not pushed toward independence, children need to be protected and nurtured.
— In a sharing family, children are raised to become independent and to stand on their own two feet and lead their own life.
— In a gatekeeping family, control is the most central aspect; children will be guided.

These differences help to understand the differences in providing for the children, but also differences in what the children like. These family structures help to understand differences in culture and to build efficient marketing strategies that allow for local cultural differences within a global framework. From past research we found that in southern countries like Spain and Italy the mothering system dominates. Germany and Scandinavia tend to be more gatekeeping minded, whilst the UK is a good example of the sharing system.

The path to independence is not always strewn with roses

Having read this, you can imagine that it would not be wise to communicate with British mothers in a gatekeeping manner. Communication in the UK should focus more on typical sharing situations and values, such as quality time, independence of the child, integration in the peer group at an early age, and being a mother as well as a woman. In the German situation, focus should be on gatekeeping values such as control, education, and rules, organised peer groups and social norms. Countries such as Spain need to be addressed in a mothering way — focusing on dependent children, peer group in-home situations, home-made cooking, and extreme motherly care and protection, for example.

It is not surprising that not only the role of the mother differs across different countries. In my own experience with interviewing children in different countries, children also appear to differ. Considering a sharing-orientated upbringing, British children tend to be quite independent. Usually, we interview children aged six and over but in the UK it is quite possible to interview children aged five in pairs. The British children are brought up to be independent by the time they are old enough to attend school. From five onwards, children spend five days a week from 9 until 16.30 at school.

The main concern of British mothers is that their children are self-sufficient enough to spend long days at school. Once the children go to junior school, mothers feel it is out of their hands. Now, the school is mainly responsible for the further development of their children.

British children are generally very polite and tend to behave well out of home but are also more progressive and turn to the peer group at a very young age. I am not surprised that the British children have so much pocket money to spend – and do in fact spend it, independently.

Children in Belgium, where the mothering system dominates, tend to be much more family-orientated. Compared to British children, they are less independent and quieter. For Belgian children, the mother plays an important role for much longer.

Dutch children, who generally grow up within a combination of sharing and gatekeeping family systems, are much more assertive than Belgian children but less progressive than the British. The Dutch gatekeeping mentality originates from the historical background of Protestantism. Protestantism is based on external and social control. Thus, the Dutch children are steered towards independence and early responsibility but within certain socially determined bounds.

Seeing these differences one should not assume that the same products and cartoons for kids would be a hit in every country. The 'Power Rangers' and 'Spice Girls' were biggest in the UK. In Belgium, 'Kabouter Plop' and 'Samson en Gert' – both regressive children's programmes – score very high. It is of great importance to check new ideas and communications in each of the countries where one is planning to introduce a product. This comes because a hit in one country certainly does not guarantee a similar hype in other countries. A good example of this is the Dutch Flippo. Although an enormous hit in the Netherlands, it did not do at all well in Belgium. In Belgium the Simpson caps scored much better. The Simpson caps were a Croky crisps promotion practically unknown in the Netherlands.

Cross-cultural balancing acts

I was born in the Netherlands, spend my childhood in the German-speaking part of Belgium, spend my teenage years in the UK and came back to study psychology in the Netherlands. I have lived there for the past eleven years. However, am I really Dutch? If you should ask me, I certainly feel Dutch. My acquaintances seem to think otherwise. The other day, when my best friend and I were chatting about when we first met, she told me that she remembered thinking how English I looked and behaved. This is in contrast with the remarks I used to get back in England. At six form college (is not the same as American University), everyone used to find me rather 'continental,' as they put it.

When you live in a foreign cultural environment, you somehow unconsciously pick up things from this country, its cultures and traditions, and make them your own. Yet, you do it in such a way that the culture from which they originate is no longer instantly recognisable. You appear to internalise certain elements that somehow seem to appeal to or fit with your own perceptions of the world. From experience, I feel that it is important that you stick to your original culture, for nothing is more confusing than not having a clear identity, a certain foundation. The best way to feel comfortable in another country is to find a balance between your own values, norms and customs and those that predominate in the country you live in.

I must say though, that it appears to be much easier for a child to adapt and enjoy living in a new country than for an adult. Looking back, I found it much more difficult to settle in the Netherlands at the age of 18 than to adapt to a new life as a child in the UK. Going to the UK now is not a holiday for me. It just feels like visiting the place where I used to live, reviving memories and experiences. Eating fish and chips wrapped in a newspaper, shopping at Marks & Spencer, having baked beans on toast, buying Slazenger deodorant and having lunch in a pub are just few of the things on my to-do list when I am back in the UK. From the moment I arrive, it takes just ten minutes and I have forgotten Holland and the Dutch.

Ask the children; the truth comes from their mouths

Could it be that children are more open to others and other experiences? Could it be that children have not yet fully developed, determined and internalised certain values and norms? So, having tried to persuade you that cultural differences should not be underestimated, I would also like to leave you with the idea that when trying to understand a different culture for marketing purposes, we should try to approach it on a child's level, without preconceived ideas but with openness for different behaviour, norms, habits and values.

Tom Meere *graduated in Political and Social Sciences. Before entering "the real world", however, he escaped for one year to Italy, just for the sake of the – esthetic – experience, but also to study the semiotics of images and sounds, and the history of Italian music.*

Back in Belgium, Tom joined Censydiam, first as a researcher at the head office, then as a member of the Censydiam Institute, coaching new staff. Today, he is part of the international team, doing research all over the world, sometimes going back to his old love, Italy, and often travelling and discovering new ones.

Tom takes us on a gastronomical tour of Italy, making our mouths water. However, Tom would not be a true Censydiam researcher if he did not show us that there was more to Italian gastronomy than just food.

Italy: the appeal of 'Mediterranean ways'

Before our story actually begins, I want you to meet someone. The man I want to introduce you to is Roberto Carluccio, an Italian cook-businessman living in England. Some of you might have heard of him, as he is slowly beginning to become a famous person with his television documentaries and his book on the authentic Italian kitchen. For those of you who do not know this man, let me just explain that he owns a quite successful restaurant in London, offering a wide range of traditional Italian dishes prepared with the help of authentic recipes. His knowledge and expertise were put into a BBC series and into a book, and sold in many countries, especially in Europe. The man has a lot of success promoting the authentic Italian cuisine and his testimonial incites people to try out whatever he proposes.

The question you could ask yourself about this, is whether the renewed success of Italian cooking and food is just another fad that will pass on in a short while. Or is it something else, a sign of the times? Some of Carluccio's statements show us where to look for an answer to this question. So, let us find out...

Changing perceptions on Italian cooking. Statement on popularity of Mediterranean diets

Mediterranean (especially Italian) diets are becoming increasingly popular with many consumers. Some time ago, people spoke about the Italian kitchen in terms of spaghetti Bolognese or osso bucco and their vocabulary remained limited to these dishes, which – by the way – were almost always adapted to our western tastes. For instance, the famous Bolognese sauce started to lead its own western life, stuffed with meat, loads of vegetables and used in huge quantities, whereas the 'real stuff' contains not even half of the quantities used over here and has a far more refined character. In fact, Italians would not even have recognised the western interpretation of this particular sauce.

More recently, people start to adapt their rough and stereotypes-based definitions of the Italian kitchen and discover that it had a lot more interesting sides to it than they initially thought. All sorts of pasta, pasta sauces, vegetables, and so on are included in the new definitions. Many new products have been introduced successfully on the market, and they seem to find their way to average consumers kitchens. In many supermarkets you will find nowadays a whole range of 'prodotti Italiani' like all kinds of pesto, funghi and cheese sauces, special vegetables, tartuffi, and more different kinds of pasta than you will ever imagine. The Italian food boutiques also become more popular. There you can find a great variety of products, from espresso coffee to exquisite olive oils and vinegar, from freshly made pasta to all sorts of ready-made meals. Of course, this goes along with a promotion of Italian kitchen design tools and pottery, like the coffee cans (Illy), Alessi stuff and so on.

Next to this process of differentiation (the refinement of definitions), we also see that the need to adapt foreign tastes to our own senses is decreasing. In other words, authenticity and pureness are values that are slowly becoming more important. Respect for genuineness now prevails over the desire to incorporate and assimilate exotics into our own habits. In a market situation, this would mean that 'westernised' products and brands are not so much wanted anymore as the real, local (imported) stuff. Just think about all the Italian A- and B-brands you can find nowadays in our supermarkets (Barilla, DeCecco, Esselunga, and the traditional brands like Buitoni and Cirio)...

So why the Italian kitchen, I hear you asking. Why not the Russian, Korean or Mexican kitchen?

Wholesomeness is one of the fundamentals. But why?

Most people associate the Italian or Mediterranean kitchen to olive oil, so let us take this product as an example of what we want to explain here. The last few years, this originally Mediterranean product has found its way to our kitchens. When it first became more popular, the most important benefit connected to the product clearly was its healthiness. It was and is believed to be one of the more 'healthy' kitchen fats available. Olive oil is a natural and pure product (*olio extra vergine*), which definitely creates a difference with other fats that carry the same health benefit (for instance low cholesterol) but that have gained this benefit in an unnatural way (processed diet products – except for products derived from olive oil, like some margarine). The combination of healthiness and wholesomeness add a lot to the attraction of olive oil with many people, especially in era where many problems with respect to food arise (scandals, genetic manipulation, and so on). A lot of people are in doubt of what is safe to eat, they start to realise that they should be more aware of what they are eating every day and from this point of view wholesomeness and basic authenticity become very attractive.

Nowadays, olive oil is also appreciated for its taste and for its contribution to the authenticity of certain meals. It is offered by many different brands (from distribution outlet brands to prestigious artisan Italian brands), all offering different tastes adapted to specific preparations. The wide range of availability guarantees a satisfying choice for all: those who are just looking for generic oil as well as consumers who are looking for more special products/brands. The Italian kitchen is seen as simple, traditional and quite accessible, also for those people who are not immediately looking for especially exotic dishes and who merely look for a wholesome and tasty variation in their menu's.

Generally, people also associate Italian food to good taste and indulgence. It is not really about extreme refinement (though it can be, depending on a person's individual motivations with respect to food), but about enjoying to the fullest a delicious yet simple, accessible and authentic meal; a real and honest meal that is intrinsically enjoyable and does not play on extrinsics or outward appearances. The honesty and authenticity of food imply also wholesomeness, which even increases its appealing power.

The Italian kitchen is more than just food...

Besides taste, authenticity, and wholesomeness, the Italian kitchen is strongly associated to a certain atmosphere, which we can describe as very convivial, sunny, and joyful. The 'Italian theme' is often used in the world of commercials to add some emotional surplus value to products. Just think of the Mamma Miracoli commercials (for instance the one where we see an ancient Asterix & Obelix family raving about having pasta that night) and you know what I mean.

So where does the appealing power of these surroundings derive from? In order to understand this, we might want to take a look at some very general tendencies in our western societies the last few years and at the role of food within these trends.

- Food habits do not escape from a *general tendency towards more individualism*, which has become visible in Western society during the last decades (since the late sixties). Family life, religion and belief, education, the global cultural offer, etc. are increasingly centred on the individual and adapted to satisfy individual needs. A lot of people want to be successful, have a great career, strive for luxury and power and they forget – to a certain extent – about family life. Cocooning in this context is not an expression of the desire to recreate family life; it should be merely considered an attempt to escape temporarily from a stressing, even hostile and threatening environment.

- On the other hand, we also notice a counter-reaction, a trend that reflects a *need for unity, and a re-estimation of human and traditional values* as a compensation for the cold and distant environment that surrounds the individual. Here, achievement is starting to lose its battle against enjoyment, and against the harmony and security offered by family life. Precisely these emotional arguments or values are felt to be present in Italian – and by extension Mediterranean – family life.

- Both of the above mentioned trends meet in the new importance attached to finding or creating a balance between individualism on the one hand, and family life on the other hand.

The evolution towards more individualism has certainly affected habits with respect to food. Time management forces the individual to limit time used for meals and for cooking, or, at least to combine eating and doing something else at the same time (working, reading, watching TV, ironing, and so on). Our speeding society causes people to look out for a solution for these timing problems. Fast food, ready-made microwave food and any product that offers a time benefit becomes useful and even attractive. The opposite trend (back to basics) obviously wants to re-install classical values and norms with respect to food, and makes time for fresh cooking and eating together with others.

The desire for diversity and variety was also reflected in the big success of exotic/foreign food. These products offer a certain excitement. The opportunity to escape from boring routines, which is until today an important benefit, but, within the context of balancing between individualistic achievement and honest, authentic family life, interest in exotic products is a little decreasing because they seem too cosmetic and polished, not very authentic and because they often are linked with ready-made meals and fast food (Aiki noodles). The need for variety, excitement and adventure is still present, but it is now more expressed in terms of honesty and authenticity than in terms of outward appearances. It is here that the perceived authenticity and simplicity of the Italian kitchen come into play.

An interesting thought in this respect is that also many young cooks today are very much in favour of preparing basic meals, instead of exquisite luxury dishes (seen in 'Trendspotting, August 99, Belgian TV).

La famiglia: an appealing emotional setting?

More than the image of the family itself (demographically speaking), the idea of togetherness connected to this is strongly appealing to many people, which – in view of a counter-reaction to increasing individualism – does not need to be appalling. The mere fact of being together with others, enjoying each others presence in a carefree way, and the idea of taking this great meal with the people you like, is often felt to be a relief, especially in a stressing and competitive environment like in our western societies.

A lot of the existing stereotypes on Italian families support the idea of care and protection and are linked to a certain kind of sociability, which we (as northern people) would like very much to copy – even if we fool ourselves by even trying. All this is part of the aspirations (with respect to food, but also with respect to other products) of many people. This does of course not mean that everything needs an 'Italian touch' from now on; we only suggest that reflections of sociability, care, authentic togetherness (no competition, no status, no explicit individualism) nowadays are strongly attractive aspects of Italian/Mediterranean ways of life.

Widespread Italian stereotypes: truth or fiction?

The well-known guardian of the Italian kitchen is typically 'la mamma', a character we are all familiar with through the widespread stereotypes on Italy. In many Italian households nowadays, you will not find a lot of these stereotypical women, though the role of the mother reigning the household is quite existent.

"In Italy, people think Jesus was Italian: he lived at home until he was 33, he thought his mother was a virgin and she thought he was God."

This is a joke Carluccio made in an interview. It seems to synthesise a few common stereotypes on Italy and its people. Especially the relationship between children (boys) and their mother is subject to mockery. Now, it is true that many Italian children remain living at home until they are over twenty-five years old. Even when they are already working, they sometimes will stay with their parents in order to save some money for when time has come to move out (which could be marriage for instance). This situation is partially caused by the economic situation in Italy and the chances for young people to find a great job directly after graduating. Still, it remains an interesting fact that leaving the safe and protective environment offered by the family appears to be a hard thing to do. Parents also (especially mothers) find it hard to let go of their children, and to see them grow beyond the boundaries of their care and protection.

The idea of the family is very deeply rooted in Italy; it is something so natural that it is seldom being questioned. The importance of the family stereotypically expressed in most of the mafia films is maybe a little exaggerated, but it certainly gives us an idea about the relevance of the issue.

Tom De Bruyne *studied Psychology, and specialized in group psychoanalysis in general and youth cultures in particular.*

He loves his wife, but also loves books, film, theater, and... train-spotting. Is he showing or proving himself – or "giving himself away" – by owning up to these hobbies? On the other hand, he might himself be alienated to such an extent that he thinks to be someone who can signify himself by these hobbies whereas not yet being conscious of more effective sublimation of his urges.

Whatever may be the case, since 1889, he has been working – rather efficaciously – at Censydiam for Kids, spotting youth culture, in which, by the way, train-spotting tends to be considered as utterly square and uncool. But then, at a mere 24, Tom already belongs to the old guard.

"Learning to think as a child is one of the most revealing things in my job," says Tom. "Again and again, I'm confronted with children's own logic and frame of reference that differ so much from that of the adults. It's amazing to see how the intentions of some of our clients' concepts sometimes are off the perception of the young geniuses we see in the interview room."

Children's own logic.
Learning to think like a child

In *La struttura assente* (1968) an introduction to semiotic research, Umberto Eco advances the proposition that one cannot see anything without a pre-structured model of analysis. Things as we see them can not get a meaning until we can set them against things we know. Things are visible only through the glasses of language as a semantic – 'meaning-giving' – system. In other words: on semiotic grounds, we can forgive the primitive people of the rain forest mistaking the arrival of a plane for the landing of the gods or – at least – of an iron bird.

This semiotic paradigm also applies to the mapping of human behavior and human thinking. There are dozens of schools of psychology, which look at human behavior through different glasses – behaviorism, depth psychology, systematics... The Censydiam model, which looks at humans in relation with others and fits human behavior in with the subconscious relations/strategies between the Ego and the others, has proved to be quite workable.

I will not try to explain the workability of the model by its commercial successes although this criterion is certainly valid: the shared belief in a model indeed implies its verity. I will prove the verity of the model by applying it to the motivational target group of 'the youngsters' with respect to their 'social environment.'

From my experience as a market researcher, I have learned that the basic motivations of this target group are largely misunderstood. I have learned that the products for this target group are often clumsily positioned and that the blame for it is put on the capriciousness of a target group that is ever so hard to grasp. By tracing out the basic motivations of the adolescents, this paper intends to arrive at a better understanding of how marketers should position their products.

Psychological model of analysis: identity and reference groups

Youth culture is all about identity. The least one can say about a youngster is that he/she is in search of an identity. The uncertainty starts at the moment youngsters begin to call into question or contest the expectations parents have for them. Until the age of about twelve, parents and the adult world are their reference group. This means that the identity of children and young teenagers is *formed by taking example from the expectations of the adults*. Parents and teachers are the ones the child trusts; they get all the credit because of their authority and experience of life.

Development of identity in childhood

Identity of the child ← Expectations of the parents

Puberty and adolescence is the period in which the certainty about what the adult world expects from the youngster is being shaken. Little by little the adolescent breaks loose from the aspirations of the adult world – parents, teachers, opinion makers... – to pursue his/her own aspirations and his/her own identity. If there is anything by which adolescents resemble each other, it surely is the search for their own identity. Until puberty, their identity was assured by the fact of being a son or a daughter.

At a certain moment, youngsters in search of their identity have to loosen themselves from being sons and daughters. In this respect, adolescence can be seen as a transitional phase between the period in which identity is determined by the parents and the period in which one is on one's own.

This obligation is a cultural precept. Everyone has to leave the parental nest and start one's own life. Our society is based on this precept of *exogamy*. It should be noticed that Sigmund Freud has always associated his famous and often misunderstood ban on incest with the precept of exogamy. In fact, Freud's ban on incest stood for something completely different from 'getting it on with your mother.' The ban on incestuous relations is indeed directed at the mother and understood as: "Thou shalt not enjoy thy child." The precept of exogamy implies a cultural obligation in that adults in the making should take their own ways and 'not be tied to mother's apron strings.'

There is of course also the influence of the peer group on the identity of children, but this can only happen as long as the parents and the adult world allows this. The parental desire is the basis for the child's identity. If this is not available, neither the peer group can have an influence on it.

Identity and adulthood

| Identity of the adult | ⇹ | Expectations of the parents |

Adolescence as a transition

Adolescence is the period in which choices have to be made. Different ways lie open to the youngster. There is an ample boundary between remaining dependent on one's parents on the one hand and on the other becoming adult. This is precisely the area in which youth culture pops up. Youth culture is a *solution of compromise* between the dependent childlike identity and the independent adult identity.

Being an adolescent is an in-between step. For one thing, it implies that one breaks loose from the dependent son/daughter identity; for another, one does not yet have to take the final step to the choices and responsibilities of adulthood. The combination between one's own choices without the many – e.g. financial – sacrifices makes adolescence into a period of its own. This period is so engaging that, today, it becomes harder to take the step to adulthood. This has two important causes.

Compulsory education until the age of 18 and the fact that an increasing number of young people continue their studies thereafter, indeed no longer allow to linger in that position.

On a wider social level, this extension of adolescence must be understood as part of the disappearance of the main signifying systems such as Catholicism and patriarchalism – the basis of Catholicism. In his paper on the origin of religion, *The Future of an Illusion* (1927), and in *Civilization and its Discontents* (1930), Freud demonstrates that the function of these signifying systems is an attempt to answer existential matters in life, to answer questions of identity – who am I? – and sexuality – how should men and women be? how should men and women conduct themselves together? – and authority – which laws do I have to obey? what is allowed and what is not? These are also the questions to which the adolescent in this transitory phase between childhood and adulthood has to find an answer. Apart from that, it is also the secret recipe of every sect: a group gathers around a sect leader who gives them – in exchange for devotion – answers to all existential questions.

Identity is recognition

In *Fonction et champ de la parole*, Lacan puts that the original function of language is not the transmission of information but a demand for recognition. Through speaking, I define myself as opposed to the other. A conclusion that is often overlooked is that any identity holds out only through the recognition of others. If I would call myself a psychologist without having studied psychology, I cannot hold this up since others will not recognize me in my identity. Even the rebel cannot be a rebel without the recognition of others; if they do not seen him as a rebel he simply is not a rebel.

At a particular point of their adolescence, youngsters stand at a crossroads. At that particular point, they refuse their parents' recognition of their son/daughter identity and have to put up something different against it. One could see adolescence a *creative process of coping* with both demands.

With respect to the recognition of their identity there are four different positions.

Withdrawal. One does not go actively in search of an identity that differs from the one founded on one's parents' expectations. One sticks to one's parents' recognition as a son/daughter.

Seeking recognition from the group. One actually searches for a new identity. The group is the best way to gain recognition. One takes part in youth culture; one displays the signals of the culture and by doing so one is recognized as part of that culture.

No active interest in the recognition by others. One does not tie oneself down to a particular culture but searches for individual satisfaction in a personal project. One does not search oneself through recognition by others but one wants to prove something to oneself.

The fight for one's identity. This group of young people fights an active fight to free themselves from the expectations of others, generally their parents. These youngsters cannot enjoy being young as they are constantly in a position of defense. The rebellion of their identity is nothing else than an implicit or explicit fight against others – against their parents, against society...

The recognition of an individual identity can thus be reduced to two dimensions: the *reference group* and the *position in relation to this reference group*. The youngsters' reference groups are the world of the parents and the adults on the one hand and the world of the youngsters on the other. Two positions are possible with respect to these reference groups: one either expects to belong to the group or one explicitly seeks to differentiate oneself, as represented in the following diagram.

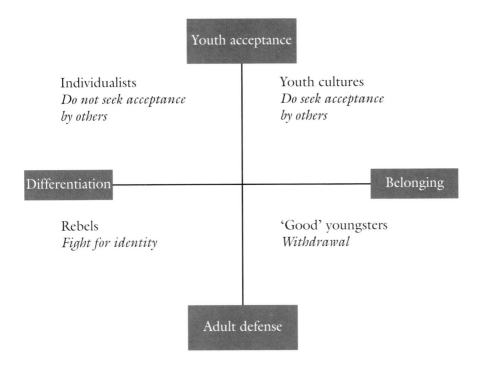

Youth cultures: methodical situation

Youngsters who seek the company of other youngsters and identify themselves with the culture of this group are situated at the upper right side of the quadrant. They are driven by a need for recognition by other youngsters. They think of themselves as youngsters but do not yet feel ready to assume the identity of an adult.

The three other quadrants distinguish themselves from the upper right quadrant by the fact that they have *no group character*. The single-minded – differentiating from the youth cultures – and the rebels – differentiating from the world of the adults – do not need the group since they have individual projects. The 'good' boys and girls – belonging to the world of the adults – do not dare or cannot in fact belong to the group of youngsters. They do not, either because their parents make it impossible or because the youngster himself/herself chooses the regressive position. Good boys and girls are in fact recognizable as a group but they do not act as group members.

Hence, if we want to look at all youngsters, we must look in all the quadrants. If we want to look at youth cultures only, then we must limit ourselves to the upper right quadrant: *belonging to the peer group*. While elaborating on this study, it appeared that serious evolutions could be found in all segments. It is clear that new forms are evolving among youngsters; a norm that was not prominently present say five years ago.

Shifts as a consequence of a change of discourse

Rebellion

Rebellion has always been seen as a typical feature of adolescence; this period is called: puberty. The youngsters question the values and norms of their parents and, during puberty, the childhood catchphrase "my dad is stronger than yours" is slightly changed into "father is an old-fashioned jerk". Well then, today we see an obvious evolution here. None of the youngsters we interviewed told us about actual conflict situations between them and their parents. Parents do disagree sometimes with their children but today they avoid a confrontation. Today, it is up to the youngster to know what he/she wants. We repeatedly heard the following statements.

A boy: "When my music is on full blast, and my father is in the mood, he just participates in the caper."
A girl: "I have two good friends; one I know since long and also my mother."
A boy: "My mother asks me when I go live apart. I say then, next year maybe."
A girl: "She is a friend, rather than a mother."

The question is: What has changed? Have youngsters become less rebellious or have parents become less authoritarian? We firmly believe that the reason has to be found in the latter. Parents today do no longer represent the 'next generation.' What do we mean by that? Up to now parents served as examples of adult life. Youngsters had to be prepared for the requirements of adult life. The parents saw to it – and what is more, they emphatically expected – that their children were educated in an atmosphere of respect for authority, for prevailing values and norms. Parents saw to it that their children became adults.

We could also say that parents saw to it that adolescence was as short as possible. It was the parents' task to make the transition from childhood to adulthood as orderly as possible. The rebellion of the youngster was directed precisely against this smooth exchange of one authority – that of the parents – for another – that of the social order with which one has to conform and which the parents represent at the time of adolescence.

The average youngster of today — the one I see in our interview rooms – does not reveal anything of this; youngsters can simply be youngsters. Parents do not prevent youngsters from being youngsters, for the simple reason that they do no longer know it in the first place. In this new age with greater freedom of movement for the adolescents, there is no place for rebellion. When there is a general oppression, the rebel is a freedom fighter. When there is general freedom, the rebel is seen as someone who is desperately seeking attention. If you are open to these things, if you are not going out to explore these things for yourself, you are not authentic.

The 'good' boys and girls

These are the so-called 'nerds,'[1] the youngsters who dutifully conform to the norms imposed by society: studying earnestly, not embarrassing the public at large, not attracting attention...

Strangely enough, however, with the rapid expansion of the Internet, the youngsters belonging to this group – who used to be bullied at school – now are no longer negatively considered by the other groups. On the one hand they have a knowledge that answers many of the others' aspirations; they are 'professionals' as regards new technologies and job prospects. On the other hand they are often perceived as being authentic: they simply do their own thing, regardless of the 'peer pressure.' A nerd is not just a nerd.

---

1   The word *nerd* and *a* nerd, undefined but illustrated, first appeared in 1950 in Dr. Seuss's *If I Ran the Zoo*: "And then, just to show them, I'll sail to Ka-Troo And Bring Back an It-Kutch a Preep and a Proo a Nerkle a Nerd and a Seersucker, too!" (The nerd itself is a small humanoid creature looking comically angry, like a thin, cross Chester A. Arthur.) *Nerd* next appears, with a gloss, in the February 10, 1957, issue of the Glasgow, Scotland, *Sunday Mail* in a regular column entitled "ABC for SQUARES": "Nerd—a square, any explanation needed?" Many of the terms defined in this "ABC" are unmistakable Americanisms, such as *hep*, *ick*, and *jazzy*, as is the gloss "square," the current meaning of nerd. The third appearance of nerd in print is back in the United States in 1970 in *Current Slang*: "Nurd [sic], someone with objectionable habits or traits. . . . An uninteresting person, a 'dud.'" Authorities disagree on whether the two nerds—Dr. Seuss's small creature and the teenage slang term in the *Glasgow Sunday Mail* — are the same word. Some experts claim there is no semantic connection and the identity of the words is fortuitous. Others maintain that Dr. Seuss is the true originator of *nerd* and that the word *nerd* ("comically unpleasant creature") was picked up by the five- and six-year-olds of 1950 and passed on to their older siblings, who by 1957, as teenagers, had restricted and specified the meaning to the most comically obnoxious creature of their own class, a "square."

Theodor Seuss Geisel. Pen name Dr. Seuss. (1904-1991) American writer and illustrator of children's books. His works, known for their humorous verse and playful illustrations, include *The Cat in the Hat* (1957) and *Green Eggs and Ham* (1960).

[The American Heritage Dictionary of the English Language, Third Edition (1992).]

TOM DE BRUYNE

The individualists

They are the ones who have a project of their own. They do not care about peer pressure. They do not care about wearing the things one should wear in order to belong to a group. Therefore, they are often the ones who are aspirational for teenagers, because they are authentic. The power of this longing for authenticity lays in the assumption the real youngsters have, that these individualists have sorted out all existential problems (identity, sexuality and authority) for themselves.

These individualists are very often the ones in which a trend starts. Everything they do and wear becomes associated with aspirationality / longing for authenticity. The large clothing retailers have understood this very well, since they recently started spotting on the school playgrounds for what the trendsetters are wearing. It is not difficult to notice them, because they are different then the others, and are quite comfortable with that.

The 'real' youngsters

The basic motivation of these youngsters is the protection of the group. By belonging to the group, with its accompanying group icons, activities and language, they distance themselves from the identity such as their parents and teachers expect from them.[2]

They are the ones who follow the trend; they are the youngsters who, in their opinions, behavior, and habits, identify with one of the mainstream youth cultures. We can easily name some of the current youth cultures to which every contemporary youngster can belong – or of which present-day youngsters carry the icons.

Geezers. You shave your head; you wear a Velcro jacket – with the inevitable bulldog design – or a soccer jersey. You become a racist, you listen to house music, and execute the accompanying dance step – called hacking. You are a geezer.

---

2   We should not overestimate the importance of parents' wishes concerning their children's identity. This may have been true in Freud's times. Today, a growing child is confronted with television, teachers, parents, friends, role models, and even... marketers. In one or another way every one of them proclaims how one should behave to be a good child. We are not dealing here with the concrete characters of the parents but with the educational discourse they – and all other representatives in their wake – hold forth.

Snobs. You wear showy designer clothes; you chat in a trendy café, sipping at a cocktail with a name only insiders know. You come together because it is good to be seen together. You are a snob.

Johnies and *Marinas.* This is the gadget youth culture. They are the ones who are only too ready to wear the icons modern idols wear. They identify with what the leading brands prescribe. Examples – from my own environment – are: a FC Barcelona shirt, a tweeting key ring, an Oxbow sticker on the rear window of the car, a tattoo-like necklace, platform-soled shoes...

Alternos. These youngsters are close to the open-sandals-and-woolen-socks generation. They are not materialistic, listen to rock music, tune in to alternative channels – which, in fact, turn out to be awfully mainstreamed. They do not find hippie clothes very important though, and prefer to drink a good down-to-earth beer...

The problem with these names is that, for one thing, they point to a readily recognizable reality while for another they imply an enormous reduction. Is what you see really what you get? Forget it! Behind this little masquerade – implying a kind of security and identification that reflects a shared group identity – is hiding an individual who cries out for recognition of his/her individuality and identity.

Marketers are always tagging one of these youth cultures. That is where we have a gigantic problem: of all the youngsters we have interviewed, not one wanted or dared openly admit that he/she belonged to a particular group. Besides, most youngsters find that wanting to present themselves as belonging to a specific youth culture in a stereotypical way is a quite ridiculous idea.

Is our subdivision of mainstream youth cultures wrong then? Not at all. These trends do exist but are nothing more than a façade that allows youngsters to belong to something at least. They may well belong but at the same time they are crying out for recognition of their own identity. The biggest mistake a marketer can make is to identify a youngster who is so alienated that he/she cannot exist unless he/she belongs to a specific youth culture and seems to be incredibly happy with it!

TOM DE BRUYNE

Implications for marketing

Adolescents do not want to be grasped by marketing. Trying to offer them a mirror of themselves from an adult position (we all have seen the so-called cool skaters and snowboarders promoting PEPSI-Cola) is installing resistance on their part. They do not want to be associated with a stereotype. Everybody who has ever had a diagnosis based on a personality test knows the feeling. Your subjectivity is being reduced to certain stereotypic factors. And you do not accept this. You are much more than that. This can be grasped the best with what Lacan would have called the divided subject. Each subject is divided and thorn between several desires. To pin a subject down to one desire is a total misconception of the subject's psychical reality. To give an adolescent subject a mirror that would only show his desire to be young and cool is an image he does not recognize. When this subject sees himself to be reduced to this adult perception of adolescence, he does not want to identify with this alienated image. He wants to be recognized as a divided subject, not as an alienated subject. Not as alienated to an image of a certain youth culture.

Talk to a fifteen-year-old in the neighborhood. You will see him and think you can tell who he is, because he is trying to express his identity by using the symbols (clothes, movements, language) of a certain youth culture. By using this (alienated) image, he is communicating to his environment, e.g. towards his parents that he is choosing a different identity than the one they had always imposed on him. However, it is still not his own identity: he uses just only another discourse, another shared image, to represent himself towards others.

Taking into account the subjectivity and the basic anxiety of youngsters

He only does this, because being different from everybody else can provoke truly existential anxiety, because you get the feeling of being all alone on the world. People do not want this loneliness, and adolescents certainly often do not want this loneliness. That is very easy to grasp. Since they are detaching themselves from parental desires in order to become an adult individual, they are on the one hand gaining freedom, but the price they have to pay is fundamental loneliness and individuality. This is very often hard to bear. That is why youngsters are so much inclined to express a belonging to a certain group culture, because this comparability with others avoids the confrontation with this existential loneliness.

That is why adults have less the need to do that: they have a cultural defined identity as a parent, homemaker, or career man to hide their existential loneliness behind. Although we see more and more adults expressing themselves with youth icons, because the shared cultural Western identity has become just one of the possible alternatives and has very often proven to be a terrifying institute.

Marketing techniques in targeting adolescents

Youth today is targeted like hell, by multinationals. They have the money, they like to spend, and they use consumption goods to express themselves and to represent themselves towards others. However, a copying of their image to promote your products equals a frustrated product manager and a "difficult target group" label on behalf of the youngsters. What does not work?

1) Trying to be as cool as they are: you're not, because they know you are just trying to be as flashy as them to get them to buy your stuff; they have grown up with commercials, so they know the tricks.
2) Being rebellious: you are stupid, because you do not need to be a rebel anymore. Do your own thing, be authentic is the device, not: fight your parents. Kids that need to fight for their rights are not enjoying being young. This image is not positive.
3) Trying to catch them on their desire to be adult: big mistake. Because the image of adulthood is boring and the values they represent have caused destruction of the planet and the environment and promote hate and violence. Furthermore: adults desire to be adolescent these days. They do not have a religion or theory that gives them something to strive for. They have to work it out themselves. So we see a glorification of childhood and adolescence, because this avoids existential problems about being adult(this is one of the main decisive components in the Anorexia rage these days).

The only aspirational image teenagers have these days is being cool by doing your own thing. This is why e.g. alternative sports are so popular these days: you can develop your own style (freestyling) and rules and big sponsors do not limit you.

Another exponent of this success formula is the success of garage concepts. The rock-artist Beck – who made his world hits "Loser" and "Beercan" literally in his garage – is an example of this, but also the enormous growth of specialized magazines or newsletters.

The Internet is one big do-it-yourself playground. Everybody can do his own thing and sometimes a small initiative turns out to be very successful – e.g. a Belgian hacker, who called himself Red Attack and who hacked the site of the biggest bank in the country is now the most wanted IT-specialist in Belgium. On a more international level, Flat Eric is the latest hype. This garage concept has grown out to be the rescuer of the Levi's jeans brand. Levi's was about to die as a brand, because it has become so common that one could not express one's individuality anymore and is not belonging to the world of children and adults.

It is actually quite logical that youth has fled into D.I.Y.-concepts during recent years, because it is the only option left, since big business is hyping the image of youth. They have got nothing left to identify with in order to be different, in order to assume an other identity than the one "the Other" (parents in particular, but society in general) has of them.

It is therefore very crucial to grasp the historical determination of adolescence. Developmental psychology had always pasted several phases on individual development; According to them, we have to go through stages to become adult. A bit like in computer games. In each stage, tasks have to be fulfilled before being able to go to the following stage. According to developmental psychology adolescence is the intermediary stage between childhood and adulthood. In this period, the child needs to get rid of its dependency of the parents, while it has, on the other hand, the time to assume an adult role with inherent rights and duties. This definition is however historically determined.[3] We do not see structural equalities over cultures, or over time.

Two examples. In Western society, during the industrial revolution, the child was regarded as a little adult. He had to work like an adult and often had the priviliges of the adult. Therefore, the child did not need to rebel or to assume something else to get free of his parents' desire. These parents had no desire towards them and these children had all the privileges they could desire (actually, they had as few privileges as their parents did, but had as many duties).
A second (cross-cultural) example is the existence of puberty-rituals in certain primitive civilizations. There the transition between childhood and adulthood is accomplished by a ritual, which is centered on the hormonal phase of puberty and leaves no room for adolescence.

---

3   Michael Mitterauer, A History of Youth, London, Basil Blackwell, 1992.

So our image of adolescence is determined by a historical context. Moreover, seeing changes within this historical context is very difficult when one is in the middle of it.

Youth cultures have existed ever since there was freedom for the adolescent. The freedom they had gained, without the restraints and demands of their parents or society, had left them with the question of how they want to be like, before they had to assume an adult identity. So adolescents have the possibility to choose from a large variety of identities. They can be anything they want to be. It is very important to stress here the fact that they choose an adolescent identity. Their parents let them have this identity, as long as they also fulfill some of their demands and desires. That is why youth cultures are usually not in the first place about being different from the parents, but about how to deal with becoming an adult. That is also why youth cultures focus on being different from other youth cultures, not about being different from what society expects. Does Western society has any expectations about adolescents? No. No need to rebel, boys and girls, the government loves you, the economy needs you and everybody wants to be like you!

Today it is clear that within Western society, adolescents do not know it very well anymore. They see adults wanting to be like them, they see traditional institutions (like marriage) fail, and they see a tendency towards individuality and hedonism. So what they lack is a future to look forward to, to long for: their desire is killed; their future is cut off. They are forced to remain adolescent, because they do not see what they can strive for as an adult. Money? No, because then they would have to work so hard, that they do not have any more time for a personal life. Marriage? No, because then they would loose part of their freedom. Kids? No, because they do not know what values to give them, or how to raise them...

Therefore, what becomes aspirational today is the image of *progressive youth cultures*. Youth cultures that start themselves giving meaning to life. This is definitely the new function of youth cultures. Not just offering an adolescent image and offering a feeling of belonging. No, today's peer groups and youth cultures want to do something: the skate or skeeler rage is a way of practicing sport the way you want. The Animal Liberation Front acts against MacDonald's, because of the fundamental disrespect for mass consumption. Newsgroups on the Internet serve as a forum for new ideas.

Is belonging to today's youth culture about fun? No, not just about fun; it is about giving meaning to life. It is about seeking out a meaningful future. That is the core message. Street style is not about baggy trousers and funny characters on your shirt. It is about doing your thing in the streets, about searching your way in the urban jungle.

The message for marketing: do not try to hype the image, but try to help youngsters do constructive things, because they are forced to sort the future out for themselves. Do not stress the regressive side of youth cultures, because youth is trying to escape from regressiveness. Instead, offer them an image of creativity and the hope and the longing to have something in the future.

This does not mean that we are sliding back to the age of the individual. This image is not aspirational either, because there is an enormous striving for warmth and belonging. Nevertheless, progressive peer groups want to do something with individual creativity.

*Why did **Wim Jan Zijlstra** choose Communication Science? "Telling that you had been absorbed in reading the newspapers was always a good excuse to be late for school," Wim Jan pretends.*

To be admitted for Communication Studies in the Netherlands you are asked to study Psychology first, during one year. Now, Wim Jan sometimes wonders if he should not have continued that branch of studies. Or maybe he should have become a musician? Anyway, in the following paper, Wim Jan tries to describe some aspects of that fascinating culture: the world of the musicians.

The culture of the musicians is fascinating from various angles. First, it is a world in which identity plays a prominent role. In pop music especially, it is not only the sound but also the attire, the hairstyle and the lifestyle of the performers that play an important role. In fact, it is the main reason for the attention young people and the media have for music culture. Secondly, it is interesting from the perspective of the musicians themselves, whose roles differ also in aspects that are not related to sound and attire.

Wim Jan looks at it from the angle of a researcher at Censydiam.

The world of the musicians
Roles and patterns in a closed culture

Da capo

At school and at the university and for a time after that, I have been part of the world of musicians – initially as a shy greenhorn who looked up at the old hands, as I saw them in those days. Gradually I grew up in that world, I got to know their inhabitants, and learned their ways. The world turned out to be not only exciting but also intriguing inasmuch as it is a world in itself. In a certain sense, people who move in the world of the musicians feel a bond through the passion they share and maybe because they feel being at the source of music that to many people is a catalyst for their emotions. This sets the musicians apart from the listeners – a feeling of creativity, elusiveness, magic and art.

The world of the musicians is not only typified by the fact that music plays a prominent role in it. Music indeed plays an important and inspiring role in the musician's world but it is quite different from its role in youth culture.

In the study for my final term paper, in which I centered on the musical choices among youngsters, I 'discovered' that the description and the names of youth subcultures are often linked with their musical preferences. Nothing new, for that matter. It is the way in which we often talk about youth in everyday live: punks, R&B's, geezers... Moreover, when other groups such as freestylers or skaters are described in the press, and in various researches, their specific preferences in music are seized upon to explain what distinguishes them from other groups. Youth culture is all about identity indeed: "Who am I? Who would I like to be?" Music, as the carrier of symbols of emotion and identity, is an essential part of this quest for identity, apart from the function as a catalyst. Strangely enough, the role the different styles play in youth culture and the way in which they can be used to describe specific groups does not always hold true for the world of the musicians. In spite of the more prominent role of music among musicians, styles cannot always serve as a basis for describing their culture correctly.

In the world of the musicians, too, we can make a distinction between the practitioners of different styles. Their passion for a specific style is often even stronger and more visible than in youth culture. The way musicians dress will sometimes reveal something about the style they usually play. Their attire indeed sends various signals that depict the group to which they belong. Still, musical preferences and the choice of a specific style are not the only ways in which the identity of the musicians is formed. This way, we would arrive at a number of stereotypes. These give us no more than a limited insight into the way in which musicians deal with musical styles and give visual form to them. In fact, we can get a much better description of the identity of musicians by the way in which they move through their culture and wish to establish contacts within this world. However, to be able to understand their roles better, let us first pursue the question of culture further.

The world of the musicians as a culture

The world of the musicians is a closed and quite small, delimited culture in which most people know each other. It is a sort of a village. To be a member and be taken seriously, one has to perform well, one has to be a practiced instrumentalist but also, and foremost, one has to know the codes of the culture. Acquaintance with the codes, role patterns and manners inside the culture make it easier to become part of the group.

The existence of this culture becomes visible when musicians meet each other outside the familiar settings such as at run-troughs, at musicians' hangouts, or when appearing on local stages. When they meet at the supermarket, in school or at work, they seem confused by not being able to feel the values of their shared culture; it is as if the missing context holds the interrelation back. This culture seems to be bounded by the right setting, in which the members of this culture feel at ease and can unfold.

For many musicians being a musician is only one of the roles they play in everyday life. For a minority of them only, music dominates their whole life. Their identity depends for an important part on music; they continue to play the role in the ordinary world. They see the world of the musicians as a sort of world apart that gives them the opportunity to escape from everyday society. Without being completely conscious of it, the role they play as musicians is a role that makes it possible to express aspects of their personalities that are different from those in the everyday world. This explains why there is such strangeness sometimes when you meet them and the margins and values that define the musicians' world are lacking: the role has to be played outside the familiar setting.

Through the years, I have become increasingly aware that the inhabitants of the world of musicians could not – exclusively – be divided into the styles they play. Neither can we divide it on the basis of the instrument they play. In fact, there is a more important difference in the way in which musicians position themselves within their musical environment. It is a difference in the way in which they try to get into contact with the other members of this particular culture. Furthermore, there is a difference between the needs musicians want to satisfy by being a member of this culture.

I have first learnt so by the way in which I got to know the culture of music in the city I grew up in. It is not so however that my experience is only motivated by being a part of this very culture. The fact is that I recognized the patterns I had observed in my former city when I began to make music in my university town. The knowledge I had gathered and my experience with the codes helped me to get the hang of the new and yet familiar culture of the musicians. It led me to the assumption that there are a limited number of roles pop musicians take up in relation with the other population.

Of course, during the years I was part of the music culture, I too changed places. From greenhorn without experience and without a network I gradually worked my way up to the spot from where I could observe and get to know the local culture of the musicians at close quarters.

Roles within the culture of the musicians

We can distinguish common and recognizable roles within the culture of the musicians. It is a group of people that shows the same pattern in the way in which they play their role within the world of the musicians.

Some of these roles are still strongly music-oriented. These roles lean strongly on symbolism that is tied to style. Others are more universal roles within a culture or a network. These roles are rather associated with social relations. Within the limits of this paper we can differentiate between the following groups:

Individualistic Instrumentalists, Style purists, Socializers, Godfathers and Progressives.

Individualistic Instrumentalists

To Individualistic Instrumentalists musical skills are very important. They concentrate on their own ability and judge others according to it. In the eyes of Individualistic Instrumentalists, the proficiency with which one plays the instrument and how well one has mastered it are the primary criteria by which they judge to what extent the musician is a full member of their world.

This group is quite strongly oriented toward technique. Playing music has everything to do with professional skills. The feeling for music and the intuition of the player can only be shown if the musician is technically skilled, too.

Individualistic Instrumentalists are rather egocentric members of the culture of the musicians. They get satisfaction from increasing their ability and gaining musical experience. They are motivated to participate in the culture of the musicians since it is there that they can demonstrate their ability to people who can give them the recognition they deserve. In their eyes, the listener, who is more often than not a nonprofessional, does not hear the difference between their excellent abilities and those of the average amateur. Besides, their culture can be a source of inspiration to test their limits and explore new musical domains. It is precisely the ensemble that stimulates creativity and enriches their musical experience.

This group of musicians does not apply itself to master one specific style but draws from varied genres. Varying the styles offers them possibility to explore and push back the frontiers of their capabilities. Individualistic Instrumentalists like to experiment with sounds and techniques. Therefore they are well informed about the newest technical developments. Trying out new sets of instruments or new effects has great appeal for them. It is so that the choice of their instrument is not inspired by a specific sound that is characteristic of a specific genre but rather by the effect of the sound, by its originality. Musicians like to attract notice because of the instrument they play. They choose expensive, exclusive labels or, quite contrary, obscure ones that only connoisseurs can estimate at their true value. Still, Individualistic Instrumentalists are sometimes attracted by the authenticity or originality of an instrument. They will almost obsessively search for that unique guitar from that special year or wax lyrical about a saxophone dating from the time they were still made by hand.

Except for their admirable command of their instrument, Individualistic Instrumentalists are not very conspicuous within the world of musicians.

They hardly experience the culture as a truly different culture. They do not obviously show the change of role; they do indeed not clearly experience the change. They perceive that there are distinct codes and characteristic types in the world of the musicians but do not really lose themselves in that world. They see the world of the musicians in a rather detached way and use the culture to achieve their own end.

Style Purists

Style Purists can be found within the culture of the musicians as well as outside it. They concentrate on one genre, and insist that this genre should be followed and performed in a style that is as pure and authentic as possible. This makes the Style Purists into a conspicuous group. Not only do they make the elements of style of a genre heard; they also show it through their style of clothing, their haircut, through their choice of authentic instruments and numerous other elements. Even when they are outside the world of the musicians, their need to give form to their identity becomes visible through musical and music-related symbolism. It is not surprising then that their living quarters, too, are sometimes furnished in a musical style.

Style Purists are into being musicians with total abandon. They form a visible group that is impossible to pass over. Within nearly all local cultures of musicians, we will come upon Style Purists. Style Purists like to congregate. They are looking for purists who adhere to the same style in the first place and then they also recognize themselves in Style Purists who support a different genre. Style Purists share the passionate relation with a genre of music, and the — often traditional — lifestyle that goes with it, though they may interpret it differently.

Yet, in the world of the musicians, Style Purists are generally self-centered. They do not like to participate in mixed events and do not mingle with other bands and artists.

A good example of Style Purists was a rockabilly group that used the same rehearsal locale as my own former band. In all circumstances, this group lived according to the laws of the genre. This was illustrated by their greased quiffs, their denim or leather jackets, by their instruments such as Gretsch guitars — the only make that rockabillies will adopt and also the only one on which the genre 'can' be played — and by a drummer who played, at the same time, a swinger and a singer. The car of one of the members of the band was a turquoise fifties limo and their fascination for

Wurlitzer jukeboxes added to the purity of their spirit. At work or out about town, their quiffs stayed greased; it was not reserved for the show.

Socializers

A notable group in the world of the musicians is that of the Socializers. In the main, Socializers are socially-skilled, spontaneous people who love to enter into contact with others in an uncomplicated way. Within the world of the musicians, music does certainly not occupy center stage for them. They feel attracted to the free expression of their identity. Within the world of the musicians, expressing their identity is experienced as desirable, normative, and pleasurable. They are people who distinguish themselves by the way they dress, by the way in which they make music, and by the way in which they are valued in this culture. Among the Socializers we often come across non-musicians, who feel relaxed in the company of musicians and enjoy the creative and artistic atmosphere.

Socializers have an open mind for musicians. People who indeed just only set foot in that world are readily accepted by Socializers. It should also be noted that beginning musicians among Socializers gain admission to this world. Beginning musicians often recognize the current rules very quickly and, besides, they do not even need to know the rules to feel at ease in this culture.

The flexibility with which Socializers move in the culture of the musicians makes them into striking and pivotal figures. They know indeed almost everyone and do not see any walls between the different genres. Musicality does not determine the way in which they value their entourage; the way in which people are open to their environment is much more important. Everyone within the world of the musicians is equal for the Socializers. The only people they look up to are the most successful artists in the local musical culture since they are at the center of the culture and give access to even more contacts.

Socializers try to find connections between the different genres and bring the players of different genres together. Socializers are also often active in indirectly musical domains. They hold a seat on the board or stand behind the bar. They often also take the initiative to organize events. They like to arrange appearances, in which they often combine different styles. In doing so, they want to give more prominence to the values the musicians share.

Godfathers

One particular group is always present in the world of the musicians: the Godfathers. They are the musicians who consider themselves the focal point of the culture. They know everybody and everybody knows them. Although Godfathers do not very often introduce new developments, they have a feeling that they are the initiators. They are not active innovators within the culture but perceive themselves as a major influence.

They see themselves as father figures for the other members of the culture. Godfathers are often 'old hands in the trade.' They know the ropes and enjoy accepting a sort of advising role. Proceeding from this role they can transmit and share their experience with the newer members of the culture. They can coach other musicians and they enjoy doing it.

Godfathers seek the confirmation of their role in the local culture of the musicians. They are always ready to give advice and constructive criticism. They like to act as trailblazers in musical culture and, with this, claim to know it as no one but them. In spite of their place at the center of the culture, they are strongly oriented towards their immediate environment. They feel entirely part of the culture of the musicians and participate in it. Godfathers themselves are deeply involved in the developments of their local world of musicians. They love to accompany them and back their talents. In this, Godfathers are in search of their paternal – or 'godfatherly' – role.

The importance and influence of the Godfathers is not always confirmed. Other members of the world of the musicians do not always perceive the role of the Godfathers as crucial. They see the Godfathers as friendly and kind but also as rather passive people. Their role is that of providing contacts rather than of influencing. In the eyes of the other members of the culture, they live on their experience and are not sufficiently in search of new ideas. The retrospective views of the Godfathers are not an inspiration to everyone.

Although not everyone sees the Godfathers as true Godfathers, they generally are appreciated as personalities of the world of the musicians. Their friendliness, their social warmth, their spontaneity, their good intentions, and their status-free attitude to life makes Godfathers into unthreatening and affirmative figures for the musicians who are in search of status and competence. For insecure members of the world of the musicians they can be an aid and a gateway. Although their influence on the visible developments within the culture is not very important –

Godfathers are rarely progressive – Godfathers are indisputable pillars of the world of the musicians.

Progressives

The Progressives form the last group of musicians: a group that often takes the lead of new developments. They are in search of their own and unique way of making music. So they usually do not try to link up with other successful movements but originate their own projects. They are actively involved with playing music and searching for places where they can perform. Around them, the Progressives often form a collective that enables them to perform their music. It can be a close-knit collective but it can also consist of people who make it possible for the Progressives to carry out a specific project.

Progressives are musically creative people who are inspired on various levels and cannot be pinned down on one specialization only. The moment they have mastered one aspect of the music, they take up a new challenge.

Progressives like to perform. It gives them great satisfaction. Although showing off is not their most important motivation, the stage is a place where Progressives really feel at home. To the Progressives, the stage is the essence of the world of the musicians. It is the place where all the elements of playing music, identity, listeners, self-development, and challenges, come together and intensify emotions. Progressives are stage animals. Of all the groups, they are the ones that are most excited before the performance. Immediately before a performance, one of the Progressives among my acquaintances was, for example, not approachable and very absent. He told me that his nerves threatened to block him. Once he climbed onto the stage, he unleashed an expressive explosion.

An important difference between Progressives and Individualistic Instrumentalists is that they come to expression in a different way. Both groups perceive it as important and want to develop themselves in their expressive modes. The Individualistic Instrumentalists' development aims at the mastery of the instrument: perfect expression can only be achieved by perfect mastery of the instrument. For the Progressives the instrument is rather a means than an end in itself. They achieve their expression intuitively, by opening their minds and letting themselves go.

Other members of the scene often perceive the Progressives as self-assured, creative and artistic jacks of all trades. They embody the magic of musical creativity that is more or less elusive and unpredictable. Progressives are greatly admired. Progressives themselves cultivate this particularity. Prestige and admiration are flattering. When they are on stage, the public is important: it indicates whether their expression comes across the footlights. When this happens it gives them a kick and a release. Not the expression in itself is important; important is what expression can bring about.

Coda

Just like every culture, the culture of the musicians has its own codes and rules. Whereas to the outside world the rules and symbols seem to be the only important things, this culture really is much more dynamic and more lively. It is a culture in which the norms and discourses are determined by the interaction between the members of the culture – by internal dynamics – rather than by norms that are more global and genre-specific characteristics – by externally determined dynamics.

Apart from musical genres and identity, the relations these people maintain with each other determine the rules of the culture of the musicians. The description of the different roles makes it clear that the needs of the members of this culture cannot be explained from the musical genre they practice. It is much more important that each member of this closed and demarcated scene plays a role and maintains relations with other musicians on the basis – or on the various aspects – of the personality they express in the world of the musicians – which is a world apart. The roles people play in the musical scene determine the dynamics of the culture.

The illustration of the culture of the musicians again demonstrates that cultures are not always what they seem. It demonstrates the necessity of gaining a deeper insight into the pillars of a culture and the motives of the members of each culture. Only when we speak the language of that culture and live according to its codes and norms it becomes possible to be integrated and accepted by the members of a national culture or a subculture.

Nils J.H. van Dam, *son of a Flemish mother and a Dutch father, was brought up on multiculturalism personified. Every day again it was evident to him that the same words or the same behavior could have a different meaning in a different culture.*

In the course of his career at Unilever and Interbrew – Nils has also been Marketing Director at Iglo-Ola and Interbrew Belgium – he constantly came into contact with cross-cultural communication. He has worked for three years in Portugal, where he endeavored to combine Portuguese improvisation with Dutch efficiency. That is how he learned that empathy was essential for multicultural communication – the same empathy that really matters with regard to preventing and controlling a crisis.

As early as at the university, Nils had a passion for research. Later, too, as a marketer, he has been searching for creative solutions within a scientifically sound context. That is why he has always been a fervent adherent of the methodology developed by Censydiam, finally took the step, and became General Manager of Censydiam Belgium.

Crisis management, or motherly care for and by companies

Clients' complaints and crisis management; though both may seem to have little to do with each other, bungling or not dealing quickly enough with a serious complaint often will lead to a crisis.

In this paper, I shall deal with the tree parties that are always implicated in a crisis: the company's management, the media, and the consumers, and describe their motivations and their interactions.

The complaining consumer: an opportunity or a ticking time bomb

It often happens that serious product defects are discovered by consumers and not by Quality Control and Quantity Assurance. The consumer who finds a defect in a product generally accepts that a firm can make mistakes — to err is human, you cannot make an omelet without breaking eggs. Although the victims' reaction can be very emotional and aggressive we can say that as a rule the consumer is willing to forgive.

The attitude of the company is crucial and will determine the further course of the relation with the consumers and the prevention of an escalation. As a matter of fact, good management of consumers' complaints offers numerous opportunities.

Complaints can be used to optimize certain business processes and can even be a source of new product or production ideas.

New research tells us that customer relations are often better with consumers for who a complaint has been resolved in the past.

Where does the consumer turn to with his complaint?

It is essential that the consumer can easily find a phone number or a contact address. The greater the gravity of the complaint, the greater the risk that in the absence of a contact number — which can be reached during the weekend, too — the consumer will turn to a third party, usually the press or the distributor.

Some companies do not bother a lot with being reachable and thereby create the first risk that matters will escalate. Accessibility obviously begins with the availability of a contact number — or address — but does not end before the right — the competent — person within the company has been found!

Being reachable in the broad sense is the first indicator of the importance a firm or brand attaches to its consumers/customers. ("Do you care?")

Basically, the complaining consumer can use one of three motivational strategies.

The Security-seekers are unsure and scared, and seek advice, comfort, and security. (A passive, regressive strategy.)
The Aggressive Complainers react in anger. They will aggressively demand material as well as psychological compensation for the distress they suffered. (An active, aggressive strategy.)
The Competence-seekers will be offended. They will use their complaint to demonstrate their own competence vis-à-vis the company and the outside world. (A strategy of active, rationalizing competency.)

Although the last two strategies (Aggressive Complainers and Competence-seekers) on first sight carry the highest risk of potential escalation, the first variant is the more risky for the firm itself.

The passive, regressive victims will be surrounded by their families, by friends — or by the media — who will take up their aggressive or competent strategy. Three reasons make it into an explosive cocktail.

A greater number of people will get involved in the problem and will form a front against the company in order to obtain satisfaction.

On top of their indignation, all those involved in the active (competent or aggressive) role get an additional motivation as protectors of "the helpless victim".

The pair aggression/regression (anger/fear, weeping, helplessness) that has been formed has an enormous media power and forms *a perfect synthesis* with the aggressive, competent strategy of the journalist. An explosive cocktail has been formed.

The reaction of the company

The consumer will very quickly decode how seriously the company takes the complaint and the consumer. ("Do they care?")

The elements the consumer applies to evaluate this are the following:

— The efficiency of the registration and treatment of the complaint;

— The perception of the status of the interlocutor;

— The actions the company proposes;

— The reaction time of the company.

The more serious the consumer's perception of his complaint, the greater is the importance of quick and personal contact.

If there are complaints about actual physical injury or health problems, an immediate personal visit by a – highly placed – representative of the company is the only appropriate reaction. Such a visit will prove that the person in charge as well as his company find that the problem is important. The person in charge himself can assess the seriousness of the damage, offer his apologies, and show his sympathy from the very beginning. (*Show that you care.*) In addition to that, he can take the products that seem to have caused the problem with him and have them examined. Immediately doing so, he avoids that they are photographed and shown in the press the following day. Finally, the representative should make a clear engagement as to what the next steps will be – such as compensating for the damage – and leave further particulars so that personal accessibility is optimized. (*The company has acquired a human face.*)

If the complaints only imply a potential risk of physical injury or health problems, there is more time but it is advisable to pay a personal visit the very same day and collect the risk-bearing products.

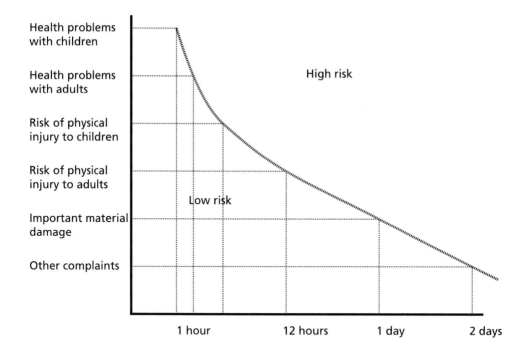

Health problems with children

Health problems with adults

Risk of physical injury to children

Risk of physical injury to adults

Important material damage

Other complaints

High risk

Low risk

1 hour   12 hours   1 day   2 days

To complaints about product defects without health risks, the company should react within less than two days.

The first reaction to the complaint is vital. The danger is still not averted yet. There are two more important steps to take.

The follow-up

The consumer always expects a follow-up. This can go from showing elementary interest ("How are things going now? Do you still have problems?") to a simple letter with an apology and eventually with feedback on the analysts' reports and the steps taken – in uncomplicated, consumer-friendly language.

In the case of serious complaints, and surely in the case of health problems, the consumer expects a quick follow-up. During the days following the incident, daily contacts are no luxury. When serious problems arise and a recall has to be made, which endangers the image of the brand, an efficient treatment of the complaint is the embodiment of ambassadors who might speak for the professionalism and care of the company in question. Bad treatment of complaints will later be reflected in the press as "I phoned but nobody has come" or "A representative of the company has come and promised to keep us informed but we didn't hear anything since".

Recall or not.
An isolated incident or the tip of the iceberg?

Is the complaint due to an isolated problem, to an unfortunate conjunction of circumstances, or is there a more general problem? Here we are at the core: "Does the company want to be caring and responsible even if it is going to cost?"

The question here is whether one wants to act like a prudent man, in a tenant-like way, as juridical language puts it. This is the acid test by which the press and the consumers will try the top management. This is not about figures and percentages – "only one chance in a thousand to get a defective product" – but about individuals and emotions: one sick child is one too many.

A company that tries to reach a compromise between profit and the risk of getting people injured and sick plays a dangerous game. The question that urges itself upon us is whether the top management indeed disposes of the necessary information to pass the proper judgment. Are there procedures by which the top management is immediately informed when important complaints are made? Last but not least, is there sufficient openness within the company so that one can make mistakes as long as one learns from it? If – minor – mistakes are not tolerated within the company – in that they block promotion prospects, for example, or result in severe sanctions – chances are that employees or staff members will hush up or try to blame others. Then, precious time and vital information will be lost.

When there is a chance of a more extensive – structural – problem that would make recalls necessary, the company can better be too careful and root out the problem than take minimalist measures and confront a problem that gets out of hand.

The white knight appears on the stage

Once-only product defects as well as structural problems may become known to the press. The journalist will assess the news value of publicizing it. The news value depends on various elements and what is more, it depends on the position of the medium at hand. Consumer's Guide magazines are interested in quite different things as the quality press or the radio news. Generally speaking, we can say that the news value is determined by the seriousness of the problem or the consequences, the proximity of the problem, the size and the reputation of the brand or company concerned, the previous history of the brand or company – have there been precedents? – and the presence of "emotionally charged material". Interesting emotionally charged material is, for example: spectacular photographs, gripping testimonies of victims – aggressive as well as regressive and emotional interviews with spokespersons – aggressive as well as evidently erring or lying...

In order to assess the role of the press, it is important to understand the psychology of the journalistic profession. The primary role of the journalist is to inform the public. It is a form of education, *a combat against ignorance*. The fact that the journalist chooses what he wants to publish and what not to publish – defining the agenda as it were – puts him in a position of power.

Some journalists – especially the investigative journalists – see their task in a broader perspective than informing correctly; they want to give interpretation, too, discover and even unravel problems, find connections between facts. They see themselves as the *protectors of the unknowing consumer*, as the *conscience of society*. With this, a critical attitude is highly important: things are not always what they seem to be!

When a journalist gets notice of particular complaints, he usually contacts the firm in question to get additional information. He will quickly decode whether the company attaches sufficient importance to the complaint and takes the consumer seriously. In addition to this, a defensive and rather uncommunicative attitude of the firm will create the impression that one tries to hide or hush up something. Moreover, the journalist feels hampered in what he considers to be his essential role, informing the consumer. We see the instant birth of a perfect symbiosis between the powerless victim/consumer and the investigative journalist, the protector of the consumer, the white knight. The hunt for the aggressor is on until he gives in, confesses his guilt, and takes the necessary measures to prevent further problems.

A company takes to flight from the press

A fundamental concept in psychological role-play with victims, journalists, and company makes it possible to think up a remedy against the escalation of a crisis.

The company in the role of the aggressor – perpetrator of material, physical or psychological damage – will be seen as cold, distant, sly, powerful, interested in profit only, inhuman; it is a machine.

The duped consumer feels hurt by the undermining of his capability or seeks to vent his aggression and criticism or wants to be consoled and get attention.

The journalist sees himself as a source of information and protector of the consumer. He is critical by nature of every institution of power — the industry included. The company that tries to restrict communication with the journalist — and with the consumer — in order not to say anything wrong or because it is "the policy" confirms itself in its role of archetypal aggressor: cold, calculating and distant. *The company that refuses to show its face positions itself as inhuman.* The journalist is stimulated in his basic motivation and uses his own weapons: he fixes the agenda and uses the emotions of the victims as a whip. He uses his sharpest pen to describe the epic combat of the powerless, human and ill-treated consumer against the powerful and anonymous evil. News value assured!

The more scathing the criticism of the press, the greater is the tendency of the company to adopt a defensive attitude and be cautious. Every word may be misinterpreted. The victims do not receive reparation or attention and the journalist's story gets more and more fresh fuel. The media attention usually brings yet more problems to the notice and rakes up old matters. This mechanism is self-fertilizing as long as the parties continue their classical role-play. In fact, the only party that has every reason to break through the vicious circle is the company.

The remedy to defuse a crisis

Getting right to the point: the stricken company must act like a prudent man in the literal sense of the word – or maybe rather as a caring housewife.

Phase #1

The company should adopt a *human face* as quickly as possible. A human face that feels concerned. A *human being* that says and shows that human suffering touches him ("that he cares"), that says that he is dealing with the problem and on his way to find a solution ("that it is important") and says that the company will assume its *responsibility* ("that the company cares"). The only person who can assume this role in a credible way is the highest person in charge.

The company should *communicate personally with the victims*: for the victims too, the company should have a human face. The victims should be taken seriously and their problems should be resolved – paying for the costs without discussion or conditions being the minimum. They should receive *attention and recognition.*

The company should adopt the role of the *underdog.* It must disembarrass itself from the domineering role of wanting to be the best and the strongest – its normal role in a business context – and act like a human company with its many problems, a company that has made mistakes but wants to learn and do its best.

The most significant argument however is that the position of the underdog defuses the aggressiveness of confrontation. One surrenders and submits.

The company should communicate with the press in a climate of openness. The company should show that it is concerned and human. It should be clear that the company will save no trouble to resolve the problems and prevent them.

Employees as well as clients and suppliers should be kept informed as best as can so that the communication and the conduct of the company are consistent.

It must be clear that it is very difficult for a company to just pretend, to stage events. The galvanized press will put sharp questions indeed, will verify statements from various sources, and unmasking would destroy the credibility of the company.

Phase #2

The company should search for possible *neutral ambassadors* who will give positive testimony of the company and who have more credibility with the press and the public such as consumers whose complaints have indeed been dealt with, victims of too strict measures taken by the authorities in conjunction with the crisis, clients of the firm and so on.

By their greater credibility and their more emotional tone, these ambassadors can certainly compensate the anger and create sympathy for a company in difficulties.

Recapitulation

Crises set in through the fact that a company has insufficient attention and care for the consumer.

The consumer reacts with an aggressive, or a competent, or a regressive strategy. These strategies form a perfect symbiosis with the basic motivation of the press.

It ushers in a role-play that forms a perfect vicious circle with only one loser in the end: the company. The powerless victim and the critical journalist, the defender of the weak and the conscience of society, begin the fight against the unfeeling and profit-seeking company, the aggressor. The gloves are off. In this fight, the bare emotions of the victims count the points.

When critical journalists put pen to paper, the reason of the company is no match for the emotions of the victims.

The company should adopt a human face. It should show that is cares for the consumers. It should disembarrass itself from the role of aggressor by becoming the underdog. Finally, the company should surround itself with ambassadors who have credibility and testify to the care and humanity of the company.

The company should change from an efficient business manager into a diligent and 'prudent man' – or woman.

*Does **Christophe Fauconnier** have real roots? The Belgians call him South African, the South Africans call him French, and the French call him Australian.*

Not only his nationality is hard to define, but also his educational background. He holds master's degrees of both Economics and Psychology. He has managed to combine both these fields well during his six-year working experience at Unilever.

There he had the opportunity to work in the Netherlands and in Belgium, getting a good feeling for both Sales and Marketing. Today his focus is the world, covering all its corners, and trying to understand humankind... or maybe is he in search of his own roots?

Reshaping the supermarket based on understanding the consumer as a provider

Historically, marketing research, and more so Qualitative Diagnostic Research, has focussed on the consumer and his relationship with a product or brand. The shopper and the satisfaction of shopping have been less the subject of study, although many facts have been gathered about actual shopping behaviour. Yet both satisfaction processes play an important role in determining the eventual buying behaviour. Where the consumer satisfactions are seen to be more the domain of the marketing experts, the shopper and the store are left in hands of sales. The fact of the matter is that a holistic approach is required to understand the eventual buying behaviour of the consumer. In this paper I will illustrate how Qualitative Diagnostic Research has served well in building up insights, which have helped the client, to development a integrated category management approach, whereby both the marketing and sales issues have been addressed.

Shopping is an act of significance coloured by needs and desires. By understanding the motivations of shopping, in relation to a particular category, a retailer and manufacturer have more ability to act upon these needs, instead of re-acting upon the shopping behaviours.

Shopper research is certainly an area that has attracted much attention (and budget) in recent years. The Category Management process has enhanced the need to collect information (data), but speed and urgency to obtain data has in some cases led to a fly-by-night approach.

The major problem has been the abundance of data and the lack of insight. Facts were gathered, but how these facts fit together was not well understood.

How does the shopper relate to the consumer? Were we studying two objects, or were we studying two acts of significance of a same individual? Where marketing knew a lot about the satisfactions and needs of the consumer, less was known about the satisfaction of shopping (providing). Yet both satisfaction processes have an influence on the eventual buying process.

What is required is a holistic approach whereby both consumer and shopper insights can be integrated. The starting point has to be the individual and how he/she gives meaning to certain acts, products and occasions. Focus is less on the brands, but more so on the product category as defined by the consumer.

The Shopper

To start with, let us first clarify what we mean with the term "shopper". In many cases the shopper is also a consumer. But in all cases the shopper is a provider. This providing act has a lot of significance. Not only for the individual himself, but also for the people which he/she is providing for. Shopping is an activity you undertake nearly every day in order to obtain goods for yourself or for those people for whom you are responsible. Although most shopping trips have a routine nature that simply repeats previous experiences we also see that the act of providing has a social significance.

The reason why we refer to the shopper as "the consumer as a provider" is that even if the housewife, who is still in most cases responsible for the shopping activity, is buying products for others, she is constantly influencing her choices based upon her desires. Indeed, if she merely bought what the other members of her household asked for, shopping would be relatively easy.

The Double Satisfaction Loop

What we see is that there is a double satisfaction mechanism that influences the eventual buying behaviour. Where a group of people can have the same desires towards the consumption of certain products and therefore have a similar preference for brand X, their shopping strategies can be quite different. Because of the utilisation of different shopping strategies, the eventual product or brand these people buy can be very different. It is not because the brand did not connect with their consumption needs, but more so because the brand did not connect with their shopping needs.

Example: The consumer has a preference for Brand X, but because there is a promotion (a gadget or duo pack) offered by brand Z, this consumer buys brand Z. The shopper in this case was seeking variety and surprise. If brand X were offering a similar promotion at the time, then brand X would probably have been chosen.

It is therefore important to understand not only the consumers' needs, but also their shopping needs.

Shopping strategies

One could easily assume that people utilise one shopping strategy per shopping trip, but what we found is that the shopping strategies that were utilised, were product category-related.

Although the shopper will have a more general shopping satisfaction and purchasing behaviour, it is remarkable to see how different this behaviour is per product category. It is important that we understand why this behaviour is so different. What drives this behaviour? The actual behaviour is only a result. The satisfactions of shopping and the significance this shopping act has for the individual are what drive this shopping behaviour. To understand the satisfactions of shopping we placed shopping strategies within the following frame of reference. Shopping strategies can be defined as either being more conservative or explorative. A second dimension is the way in which shopping is experienced. Is it pleasure-oriented or control-oriented.

Conservative shopping behaviour is dominated by the need to be sure of the choices that are made and they are coloured by strong elements of care. People who utilise shopping strategies of this nature, tend to be very sensitive for preferences of others, but also need a lot of affirmation about the acceptability of the product they buy. Their shopping behaviour is driven by a strong awareness of their social surroundings.

A second category of shopping strategies are strategies that are driven by the desire for control. Here we see people being as functional as possible about their shopping process and they try to either use one criteria for choosing the price, for example, or plan their purchase so fully that they put everything on a shopping list and very rigidly stick to this list. These provider do everything possible not to be drawn into impulsive buying acts and actually prefer certain stores that respect their need for control.

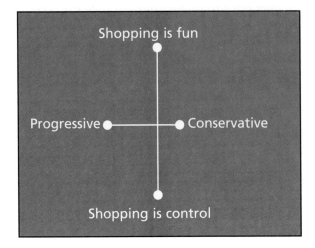

A third category of possible shopping strategies is a category in which people actually show how capable they are at shopping. They often are very calculating and smart about their shopping process, and cues that accentuate value for money of special offers are attractive for providers that are driven be these shopping motivations. These strategies are more progressive in the sense that there is an active search for newer and better offers.

A final category of shopping strategies is a category in which people seek more variety and fun in their shopping experience. Here the provider is pretty confident about the product category and what he is looking for is either novelty and/or surprise. These shopping strategies are also characterised by their impulsive nature.

Although these strategies can be seen to be universal and applicable across product categories, it must be clear the nature of the product category will determine which type of shopping strategy will be used more frequently. The type of explicit form these strategies will take will also depend on the nature of the category.

CHRISTOPHE FAUCONNIER

Defining the product category and the nature of the category

A product category can be defined in several ways. Retailers and manufactures have traditionally defined a product category based on product characteristics like wet sauces or dry sauces, frozen foods or ambient foods etc. Another way of defining a category is consumer perception. Look at the world of the category from a consumer perspective, not the world of the consumer from a category perspective.

The consumer sooner tends to group products in human-need clusters and less in keepability formats or product characteristics.

The starting point is the consumer and the need state(s) in which a certain product category can serve to obtain a specific satisfaction.

Example: When looking at Ice Cream Desert Cake in Belgium, we found that people were grouping these Ice Cream Desert Cakes with pastry and normal cakes and that these products were viewed to be the competitive field. People were describing these types of products as family treats that are best consumed at convivial moments. However, because the Ice Cream Desert Cakes were not placed in the vicinity of the normal cakes, they were often not considered during the buying process.

Another example is ice cream bars. They are viewed to be part of the Sweet Snacks product category rather than the Ice Cream category. The competitive field for ice cream bars is more often candy bars than other ice cream products.

Now, if we compare these two categories, being Sweet Snacks, which satisfy the need for fun and excitement, and the Cake category which fits well with the need for convivial family sharing, it should be clear that the way these products are presented should be different.

Therefore, re-defining a supermarket based on consumer-need states will require the following:

1. Define a product category based on consumer needs and understand the nature of this category
2. Understand and map the possible shopping satisfactions that are relevant for the category
3. Understand the presentation cues relevant per shopping strategy and per category.

Once these points are understood it is possible to develop a category plan that connects with the consumer needs and also caters for the multitude of shopping strategies.

Example: It should not be surprising that you can find a product like soft drinks in multiple places in a supermarket, presented in multiple manners. In the soft drinks rayon the product is present for the more control-oriented buyers, but along the route of the shopping trip the more impulsive buyers, or explorative buyers, can find inviting offers targeting them. Finally, at the counter, the opportunity for immediate gratification is present in the form of an ice-cold drink.

The benefit of Qualitative Diagnostic Research

Qualitative Diagnostic Research is by nature a methodology that recognises the individuality of the consumer (or provider). The starting point is always the individual and how this individual gives meaning (significance) to his surroundings.

Marketers recognise that needs and desires drive consumer behaviour, but when speaking of shopping they speak of shopping processes and buying behaviour.

We put that shopping behaviour is also coloured by needs and desires and must also be explored and understood in this manner.

The way in which we do this is by accompanying the provider to the store (her store) and letting her do her normal shopping trip. Later in the day, or early the next day, this provider joins us for an in-depth interview, whereby we reflect back to the shopping trip and try to get an understanding of the meaning which this provider gives to her shopping acts.

Although we are aware that talking about the actual shopping trip is a reflective process, whereby people tend to rationalise their behaviour, we use techniques that focus on uncovering the desires and motivations of the shopper. Actually, the shopping trip of the day before only acts as a stimulus to facilitate the interviewing process. This does not mean that no lessons are drawn from the accompanied-shopping process, but that these lessons are more of an explicit nature.

Not only do we try to understand the shopping strategies that people use; we confront them with actual products whereby they can reconstruct the shelves in the supermarket. During this reconstruction process we unravel the criteria people use (which are not always rational) to group products and we focus on how these product groups fit into the lives of the provider.

Qualitative Diagnostic Research has as main objective to generate hypotheses, but also has the advantage that you are speaking to a subject, whereby answers can be understood within their context and within this individual's frame of mind.

The greatest benefit has been that we have been able to understand better the complexity of shopping and can offer the client a more complete picture, whereby the world of marketing and the world of sales have found common ground.

Qualitative research enriches us with the language of the provider and the diversity of options, which are crucial to create a platform necessary for a metric follow-up. What we experience is that this type of research brings us insight, and the metric follow-up brings validation and quantification.

Implications for the brands

Kotler first presented the P's of marketing and one P referred to the P of Place. The place in the store, but also on the shelves, has not been the major concern of the traditional brand manager, yet the place a brand or product has on the shelves has an important significance for the provider. The provider is constantly looking for cues that enable his decision-making process, and although he arrives at the store with a lot of preconceptions, the shelf is an important source of information. Like people, the company it keeps will affect the image of a product (or brand). A manufacturer must therefore think well about shelf placement.

Another implication is that a brand must not only work to maintain consumer loyalty, but must also understand the shopping strategies of their core consumers. It is not because a consumer shows changing behaviour, that he is not a core user, but more so that his shopping needs are not always addressed. Great brands have the ability to create loyalty, but also need to have conquering ability. To do this they need to connect with the shopper and the consumer.

When she first encountered market researchers, **Annemie Cordemans** *found that they were an odd bunch of psychologists and sociologists, crack-brained artists, half philosophers, yet half executives.*

Annemie has been a market researcher herself for 14 years now, first in New Zealand, then – since five years – at Censydiam. The birth of her son kept her near home for some time. Meantime she became increasingly involved in more specialized qualitative research: more complex motivational and perceptual studies, explorative and creative studies, new types of studies such as category management.

Since one year, Annemie is Corporate Researcher Special Projects, which brings her into contact with people in every branch of the worldwide network of Censydiam. An excellent opportunity to put that odd bunch through the same mill as Censydiam does with consumers.

Old poachers make the best keepers, or: researching market researchers

Everybody knows what Censydiam and other market research bureaus do and the role they play in society and economic life. We research what motivates consumers in the use of products or services. We research their purchasing behavior. We research how manufacturers can respond to it, and how to position and display their products.

Censydiam also regularly assesses the needs and motivations of people in their professional life: what is the significance of their profession, what motivates them to follow that particular profession, how do they deal with it, what satisfaction do they get out of it...? In this way, Censydiam has found out, among other things, what motivates medical practitioners to take up the profession. We found out what different types of employees we can distinguish among the staff in banks, what inspires people who work in the catering industry to start a business and how we can differentiate their typologies... This information and insight enables companies and organizations to tune in more efficiently to the needs of different professions – which strongly influence consumer behavior – and approach the market in a more optimal way.

However, has anyone ever asked what motivates market researchers to practice their profession? It is high time researchers take their turn to be researched. What will we discover? Maybe we will find out that market researchers in fact are rather unsure or very controlled, that market researchers are a little disturbed, mentally, or even mad?

Some of my colleagues made an occasional — rather playful and fragmentary — attempt to diagnose ourselves. Certain company directors jokingly asked us, when we unfolded their employees' professional lives, "And what would motivate you? Voyeurism? Having control of your fellow men?" Just like them, I have always been attracted to find out — rather cynically, I must admit — what stimulates my colleagues and myself, what sort of 'mysterious' satisfaction we can find in such an in-depth investigation of the consumer market. In the following paper, I would like to lift a corner of the veil.

I base my reflections on observations I made during the many years I have spent in this occupation, on conversations I have had with my colleagues, and also on personal experience, knowledge and scientific literature. All this has given me a first conception of a typology of market researchers. Yet, this is not a profound and systematic analysis and it is even less so a large-scale quantification.

My only purpose is to give an introspective reflection and to formulate some psychological hypotheses regarding our profession. In some ways, it may perhaps help us to practice our profession better. It may also help marketing people to choose the particular type of researcher they prefer to work with. It may help Censydiam with the selection of new candidates... But let us first consider this as a conceptual exercise that is interesting and jocular for me and for the reader — which in itself is already typical of market researchers...

Researching market researchers: what does drive them on?

Market researchers have a lot in common with other researchers of all sorts, in the first place with those who do research in the field of social, psychological and social-economic sciences. Just like psychologists, psychiatrists, philosophers, etc., they try to find out how their fellow men function within society. They try to dissect and understand the conduct, the emotions and the deep-down drives of people. They try to analyze problems in this sphere and formulate solutions. Just like scientific researchers — neurologists, biologists, physicists... — they try to discern mechanisms and patterns, to draw up theories, to make a diagnosis and find new and better answers. Just as the artists do, they call the world, their lives, and their experience in question in search for creative expressions and solutions.

Why do researchers always need to question and unravel things? Why are they so restless and always unsatisfied, why do they not simply accept things as they are? A very fundamental question. Are these constant curiosities, this questioning, and this ceaseless search for answers not something of all time? Even the smallest child today pesters its parents with "Daddy, why do apples grow on trees?" — "Mommy, why do you cry?" ...

Other researchers before us have been dealing — directly or indirectly — with this "question about questioning" which is so fundamental for humankind and its culture. Their analyses confirm my observations and the reactions of my colleagues: our curiosity, our urge to analyze things, has everything to do with the need to understand things around us better, to comprehend the external world and thus master it. By making abstraction of certain phenomena, by conceptualizing reality in schemes, theories and symbols, in sum, by gaining insight, we can also gain control of the external world, which is threateningly big, complex, and chaotic. Thus we can organize it better for ourselves and keep things more manageable.

Thanks to this intelligible order, we can overcome our existential fears and uncertainties — which are inherent in our existence — and even, creatively, discover new contexts and solutions and make progress. In the end, this offers us better chances of survival and viability, more footing and — emotional — assurance in our lives. When a market researcher understands how the consumer 'functions', why he does what, how a marketing problem can be resolved, and so forth, this insight, this diagnosis gives him a feeling of ascendancy over the world — indeed! — which enables him to deal with it better and allows him to effect his purpose.

In his book 'The Dynamics of Creation,' Anthony Storr expresses it as follows: "Schemata, philosophies, religions, scientific theories and even aesthetic prejudices, can all act as bulwarks against the basic anxiety which we all suffer when we realize how large and how indifferent the world is, and how small and helpless is each individual in it... Perhaps what visual artists [and market researchers, too] are about originally derives from a basic drive to understand and grasp the world through insight [thanks to market research]. It is an extension, therefore, of the exploratory behaviour so characteristic of primates..." In his book 'Icon and Idea,' Herbert Read says: "What man always desires is a firmer grasp of reality. That is a direct consequence of his insecure existence, of his cosmic anxiety."

Insight in human motivations and market mechanisms can even be a means to grasp one's own inner world, one's own psyche better and to regulate it. Not only I myself but my collaborators also come to the conclusion that gaining insight — analyzing and finding solutions, bringing order and equilibrium to the world — also helps to overcome certain inner tensions that one experiences, to overcome certain insecurities and frustrations that one has to get over, which is echoed by individual researchers and thinkers. We are all burdened, ever since our earliest childhood, with a sort of unsatisfied, restless feeling inside, with all sorts of deep-seated fears and chaotic doubts, which we can balance or control by researching and fathoming things.

Insight in and thus control of others and the world around us can even lead to reflective self-insight and thus management of our own psychological functioning. Through the abstractions a market researcher makes about how others function, one can get rid of certain tensions and disquiet, and one can better regulate — control/integrate — one's own emotions. Bringing order into the world, finding solutions, brings a sort of satisfaction, relief and quietude in the market researcher's inner self. There you are! Research can almost be therapeutic for the market researchers themselves! In his book 'The Dynamics of Creation,' Anthony Storr defines the therapeutic effect of scientific and creative work as follows: "We are also faced with the problem of understanding, coming to terms with, and mastering the inner world of our own psyche... Harrison Gough puts it well when he writes: 'The work of art, for example, reorders and brings into balance the tensions of form and space, and in so doing moderates the inner tensions of the observer, giving him a sense of encounter and of fulfilment.' Just as the discovery of a law of nature brings with it a sense of mastery and the possibility to further advance..., so the discovery in art [market research] that there can be a logic and symmetry even in the language of the emotions makes us feel that we have some power over our own unruliness, or at least that our feelings need not be totally chaotic."

As I said before, every right-minded person, even a growing child, has this inquisitive urge, this need to learn and to gain insight, and thus to control the external world and regulate one's own inner life, in order to feel good and find one's place in society. The fact however that researchers, and market researchers in particular, put these questions ceaselessly and by virtue of their profession, leads us to the assumption that, more so than the average person, they feel the need to master life and control it.

Are market researchers more inquisitive then? Do they somehow have more tensions, stronger emotions or deeper-lying fears? Do they have a greater need of control because of the fact that for them life and the world around them is more of a problem? We should think so... Who does not remember the popular saying that it are the psychologists, psychiatrists and psychoanalysts who have the most problems with live? That they have chosen the profession to resolve their own psychopathologies? That they have the greatest problems with the education of their own children? This is probably a truism... The reader will not be surprised then to learn that many market researchers, too, are people who come from disciplines such as psychology, sociology, philosophy, and communication. However, it is not true that we would not make a good job of our work just because we would be subjected to more tensions and disquiet. Quite contrary, just because we are so unsatisfied and emotionally turbulent, because we have a stronger need for grasping control, we possibly make a better job of it. The best artists are often said to be the most frustrated artists...

The question, however, of what motivates the market researcher is not quite settled yet. What is the difference between market researchers and other researchers? Psychologists aim at discovering the psychopathological side of people, philosophers look at the existential aspects of life, and medical people study anatomy, while other scientists explore inorganic matter. Why are market researchers looking for 'the market', in other words: what is the surplus value specific research of the consumer market offers them? Indeed, the specificity of market research is that it is about social-psychological research of non-pathological forms of human functioning.

Market research deals with relatively normal human behavior related to everyday social and economic functioning. Market researchers are interested in ordinary people, in prevailing social trends. In that sense, we could say that what characterizes market researchers is their pursuit of normal life. It gives them more insight in and more control of everyday life and allows them to function and integrate better in society. The fact that market researchers follow a profession that is integrated within the general economic cycle supports this idea. A market research bureau deals with the problems of the commercial – and sometimes the sociological – world and in that sense is entrenched in a wider social context. So, at the end, market researchers are not at all that pathological as some people suppose or suggest. Although we sometimes seem a little complex or crazy, we are certainly not abnormal or mad. Otherwise we would not be able to do research with normal consumers, to formulate socially adapted solutions or deal efficiently with clients – we would have been confined in an asylum... While it is true that our work can be a personal means to come to terms with a more intensive and turbulent inner life, it also enables us to 'normalize' ourselves.

A possible typology of market researchers

Market research allows us to detect the common, primary meanings and needs that lie at the base of the use of specific products and services. It also shows us that different consumers can deal in different ways with those products and services. Consumers give evidence of alternate motivations and needs, depending on their social context, their personal histories, and the structure of their personalities, or on the situations in which they find themselves. In sum, our research gives evidence of different consumers' segments or typologies.

When we research people's perception of their professions, we can also distinguish certain typologies. We see, for example, that one may follow the profession of doctor for different reasons, or deal with his patients in different ways: some doctors will be more patient-oriented from a greater need for social commitment and empathy; others will be more fascinated by scientific research and try to minimize the relation with their patients from a greater need for self-control, and so on.

Well, it turns out that the same typology is possible when we observe market researchers more closely and compare their differences. It is clear that there are different types of market researchers who correspond to particular personality profiles, who put particular needs to the fore when doing research, who hold different functions, and so on. Consequently, their relations with the respondents/consumers and clients/marketers will also be different, with all the consequences that we already suggested regarding contact with clients, interpretation of the job et cetera.

I will try to make a sort of personal draft of a certain number of prototypical types of market researchers. I grant that, to make the draft as articulate as possible, I sometimes pushed the descriptions to the limit, to the point of caricatures – and that is why I also illustrated them with cartoons. I suspect that the reader who regularly mixes with market researchers will indeed recognize certain types. Colleagues will recognize other colleagues or themselves. For marketers, this typology will perhaps be an eye-opener and perhaps give them food for thought when they negotiate on research work and are looking for a suitable researcher...

The Energetic Explorer

Characteristic of this type of market researcher is his – or her – very dynamic, eager, and inquisitive nature. He engages in market research because he is fascinated by the exploration of the world around him, because discovering unexplored things is what motivates him. Analyzing people and their hidden motivations satisfies his sense of adventure and suspense. Uncovering new problems time and again satisfies his strong need for change and progression, and for self-expression. It enriches his life, and hands him the advantage of being able to develop his mind and broaden his horizons. Exploring the objective world allows him to vent his strong inner tensions and restlessness. It relieves his mind and gives him a feeling of liberation. Freud would have found him a healthy type who knows how to sublimate and to project himself in the external world...

Since research can teach him so many things and give his life new perspective, this type is an enthusiastic and enterprising market researcher. He tackles problems with energy and optimism. He is good at working independently. He does not easily give in, even if the assignment or the subject is a tall order. As he likes change and self-development, he enthusiastically tries out new methods and breaks new ground. The 'Explorer' is often also an explorer in the literal sense of the word: he sees it as a challenge to engage in international studies that allow him to bury himself in other cultures and to discover new behavior patterns. However, on the home front, too, he is bursting with energy. He can put in long hours and still go out for drinks with colleagues after.

Speaking of colleagues, this type is characterized by a very open and direct, easy-going association with his colleagues, and respondents. His contacts with respondents are very spontaneous, and to his teammates, he is a stimulating colleague. He also is very independent, and needs little confirmation from others whereas he himself very often encourages others. In that sense, he can function perfectly as an inspiring head of a team. In his relations with clients, we find a similar attitude. His relations with clients are outspoken and positive. He takes things in hand in a dynamic way. He is, as we have already suggested, an interesting market researcher, especially when renewing and explorative studies are concerned.

As we can see, this type of market researcher has many strong points. Yet, we can also list a certain number of characteristics for which one should perhaps beware when dealing with this type. Just because he is so enthusiastic, this type may sometimes be a bit careless and superficial in his approach. His impetuosity makes him sometimes forget relevant items or important details. His directness may sometimes come across as overpowering and, to respondents, as threatening. Although he may be inspiring as a team leader, he may miss the necessary constancy and structure.

The Faithful Friend

This market researcher can be typified as socially orientated, as an amicable and harmonious individual with a full measure of empathy. He has chosen to be a market researcher because it gives him the chance to put himself in the world of others, to connect with what goes on around him, and to participate in it. Dialoguing with consumers and fathoming and understanding what is in their minds or hearts answers to his need to integrate the objective world better, to bridge the gap between him and the external world and to feel securely integrated with a broader social context. It also provides him with a deepening of his inner life. It gives his emotional life more warmness and intensity and makes it more rewarding. Being able to find connections and solutions also satisfies his need for equilibrium and creative aesthetics. It balances his inner psyche and social tensions and gives him a satisfying quietude and feeling of harmony. Freud would perhaps have called this type the 'oceanic type,' the type that knows how to realize his childlike fantasies and his need for harmony in his contacts with the objective world ...

Concretely, he is a market researcher who practices his profession with love, with dedication and composure. He is particularly interested in the social contacts his work opens, especially with respondents and colleagues. He is very cordial and empathic in his dealings with consumers, who feel welcome and understood. Because of his social and beauty-loving character, he is especially good at guiding group interviews and generating creative material. He likes working in an amicable team spirit and is supportive and good at working together with his colleagues. That is why he likes to be part of a team and sometimes chooses to accompany and instruct younger and less experienced colleagues as a team leader. Wherever necessary, he will dash to help and to resolve the problems as a team. He is also very social and cordial in his dealings with clients and tries to immerse himself in their problems as deeply as possible.

The weaker points of this type of market researcher are an occasional lack of perseverance and nerve. He does not easily venture into new fields and when people deal with him too roughly or in an unpredictable way, he is sometimes thrown off balance. When things become difficult, he may lack the necessary energy to carry on. He is not always able to cope with the tensions and frictions within the firm and is sometimes bothered by the harsh reality of the marketing world. Sometimes indeed, he sees things too much in an idealistic way.

The Headstrong Perfectionist

Another type we regularly see among market researchers is the individualist who is illustrated by a strong character and firm determination, and who shows signs of intense passion and a high degree of orderliness, to the point of being disciplinary and perfectionist. This type gets satisfaction out of market research because it gives him the possibility to discover the laws and patterns of human behavior. Thus he can produce order out of chaos and take control of the elusive human psyche and of his social environment.

Having insight in and giving structure to chaos gives him a strong feeling of power and security. It makes him feel that he can dominate the world. It also helps him rule his very turbulent and restless inner world with the rod, and even to repress his considerable existential fears. His need for structure and order is sometimes so extreme that it becomes obsessive. He always wants to have a better grasp of people's motivations, of what happens in society, to get a feeling of being fully in control. Then he feels self-assured, capable, and in authority. Freud might have called this type the 'anal' or the 'sadistic type' of market researcher. Psychoanalysts in general would classify him as the 'obsessive' type...

When this type of market researcher makes a study, marketers can be assured that it will be profound and perfectionist. He carries out his research scrupulously and will leave no stone unturned. He will make meticulous analyses, in great detail, to make sure that he has looked at it from every angle. This type of researcher also guarantees that his report will be perfect: he leaves nothing to chance and makes double sure. Since his own urge to provide orderly insight is so strong, he will sometimes research or describe more facts than the client expects. Hence, he must be a type with stamina, immune to stress, who can work long hours until he is sure to have the solution and until his report is completed as neatly as possible. Some will call him a workaholic because he cannot let go of his work. This market researcher excels with studies that ask for a high degree of detailed examination or great depth or have a rather specialized character.

To consumers, this type of researcher may be a pain in the ass for he is very insisting and does not give in before he gets an answer to his questions. Although he knows how to deal with respondents with empathy, he can come across as rather hard and threatening. To those clients who themselves make high demands and want all the details, he is quite a relief. As we said before, those clients can be assured he will deliver thorough analytic work.

Nevertheless, the Headstrong Perfectionist is not always the most cooperative researcher and shows signs of competitiveness with the client. Colleagues can learn a lot from him and if need be he will gladly help a loyal colleague. For the rest, however, he remains rather individualistic and may come up with rather patronizing remarks. For people who work under his supervision he can be very strict and demanding — just like for himself. He will then start splitting hairs or demand that they do even more than their utmost, which can be exasperating.

Hence, this Headstrong Perfectionist has quite a few strong points when it comes to researching. His main weak points however are his extreme analytic and perfectionist tendencies, which can lead to insufficient globalization and perspective, and can work out badly in some cases. In addition, his craving for perfection can lead him to wasting precious time. His timing gets often out of hand, interviews tend to overrun their schedule, deadlines are not respected or only at the last possible minute. His longing for order may waste a lot of energy, too. His lack of rest for mind and body makes him underachieve and, as we said before, he is not the most pleasant character for people with who he collaborates, as he is regularly tense and ill-tempered and often rather conceited.

The Gentle Romantic

Another type we sometimes find in market research bureaus is the mild-mannered, unassuming market researcher who is very delicate and subservient. This romantic, dependent type likes market research because it allows him to transport himself into a different world, to flee, as it were, into a fantasy world. By transporting himself into the world of the consumer, he can forget, in a certain sense, his own reality with all the uncertainties, problems and pain it brings with it. By projecting his fantasies in psychological patterns and creative constructions, he can put the harsh realities of everyday life away from his mind. For him, working on human emotions and intuition is something very much like poetry, in which he can express his childlike naivete and fragile emotions in a safe way. That will make him feel more confident and secure and enable him to defend himself against depression and pain, and, so to speak, find comfort. Therefore, he is very sensible and empathic with his social environment. By doing market research and conceiving ideal products for the consumer, he even hopes to be able to do something worthwhile for his fellow men and to create a better, safer, and more peaceful world. He has something of an altruistic do-gooder. Freud and other psychoanalysts would call him the 'oral-infantile' or 'masochistic type,' with a propensity for depression...

Apart from that, we find that this type of market researcher is also very devoted and docile. His need for security and safety makes him inclined to carry out his assignments willingly and carefully, with the intention to please his superiors as well as the clients. Hence, he will work hard if requested. In this sense, he is also a good colleague who never fails to be supportive and will rarely if ever criticize. After all, he fears rejection, he fears exclusion, and will at all costs avoid feeling alone.

However, this market researcher also has his weaker spots. His tendency to escape into dreams and emotions constitutes a danger. It can lead to highly imaginative interpretations that do not always agree with reality. The danger is that he loses himself in irrational and fantastic constructions or disconnected concepts in which he believes himself, for the simple reason that he is totally wrapped up in them. Another drawback is that he is quite unsure of himself sometimes and, not infrequently, has problems with working independently and making final decisions. It is also possible that he feels powerless, low-spirited and depressive, incapable of going to the bottom of his study. Therefore, needing support himself, he will be of little help to his colleagues. He may feel incapable of dealing with the stress at work or with the clients' requirements. In the end, he may even drop out.

The Cynical Critic

This market researcher is typified by a full measure of aloofness and skepticism. On the one hand, he is reserved and introverted, on the other hand he comes up with biting remarks. He sees things in a realistic matter-of-fact way, quite coldly. Considering his attitude of aloofness from his environment, why does he involve in market research, why do we find him among market researchers? Well, the insight market research gives him by analyzing people is the ideal way for him to keep the world at a safe distance and at the same time gaining control of it. Market research offers him the possibility to understand his social environment rationally, to make an abstraction of it, whereby the external world becomes less chaotic, and less threateningly close. Indeed, he does not like the world – and all too often does not like himself either. He does not want to let himself go; it throws him frighteningly out of balance. On the other hand, market research offers him the possibility to link his inner world – which is so far apart from the objective world – with this external world. Dealing with it in a cognitive and critical way, and structuring it, makes the external world less threatening. Market research enables him to bridge the gap. Market research also enables him to build often very ingenious and complex structures and theories. As we can see here a strong discrepancy between the inner and the external world, psychoanalysts would probably classify this type as the 'schizoid type'...

Considering his rational coldness and cynicism, considering his lack of interest in people and ordinary, everyday life, this type of market researcher is not very suitable for routine dealings with consumers. Accordingly, we see that this type of market researcher is often better suited for quantitative research, which allows a more detached and down-to-earth attitude. This does however not imply that quantitative researchers are not be found among the other typologies, on the contrary. Thanks to his critical mind, he is capable of making outstanding data analyses but he may ruin all that out of a gut feeling – of which he has very little in any case as it threatens him. He deals with clients in a dry and nonsensical manner but, on the other hand, he is efficient and goes right to the point, with an almost mathematical precision. As a colleague, he is rarely available or accessible except when he can distinguish himself by his caustic humor and sarcastic remarks.

The Expansive Businessman

The last but not the least important market researcher I can clearly distinguish is the type of the 'Expansive Businessman.' A highly developed spirit of enterprise and urge for expansion typify him as a person. He is quite progressive and wants to grow in order to acquire status and authority. For him, market research is as good a way as another to realize this — he could do it by this means or another, in some other profession. He is a market researcher because he does not only gain more insight but also more power and can compete with colleagues. He hopes market research will help him secure a high social position and earn a lot of respect. He has a paternalistic attitude. He aims at gaining an important market position for himself and for his firm. It makes him feel capable and powerful. Actually, he asks for nothing less than to become, or be, a manager of a research bureau that incessantly expands and becomes increasingly prestigious.

He can indeed fulfill these needs, not so much by doing market research in itself but by directing a market research bureau. He possesses the driving force to lead, to urge others on, and achieve his aims. He wants to move forward and accomplish things. In that sense we have here a person who primarily sees the business aspect of the commercial world. He clearly sees his clients' interests and in the long run those of his own firm.

Although he certainly has excellent communication skills, also on the level of ordinary consumers, and even if he is capable of gaining profound insight, his talents first lie in the area of directing his collaborators. Respondents find him too imposing and immediate collaborators sometimes threatening. For his clients he is the eminent commercial contact, the person who gives direction to the project, but he better leaves actual research to his collaborators. While he is competent enough to comprehend and interpret the research data with respect to their commercial and strategic meaning, he is too impatient and too dominant to do real in-depth research in the field.

A schematic outline

Just like we do in other studies, we can go further with our analysis and explanation of what drives market researchers, in view of their fundamental individual and social dimensions, represented in the following diagram. In the meantime, the reader will have understood that all of us, market researchers, indeed need structure and order.

First, there is the *individual dimension*, represented on the vertical axis, which indicates in which manner the market researcher deals with his profession — gaining insight - personally and inwardly:

— On the one hand he can immerse himself in the world of the consumer, empathize with him, and in this way express his inner restlessness, achieving the right balance (= expression).
— On the other hand he can try to control the market environment and in this way keep control of his own tensions and fears, and calm them down (= suppression).

Then there is the *social dimension*, represented on the horizontal axis, which indicates in which manner he deals with his profession within the external, social world:

— On the one hand, proceeding from a more progressive attitude, he can — within the scope of his profession — express a strong, affirmative ego-identity, and focus on personal expansion and success.
— On the other hand, proceeding from a more regressive attitude, he can center his social feelings and sensitivity on his surroundings, striving for social acceptance and protection.

The following diagram visualizes these two dimensions and the four poles. I have also indicated the positions of the different types of market researchers I have found.

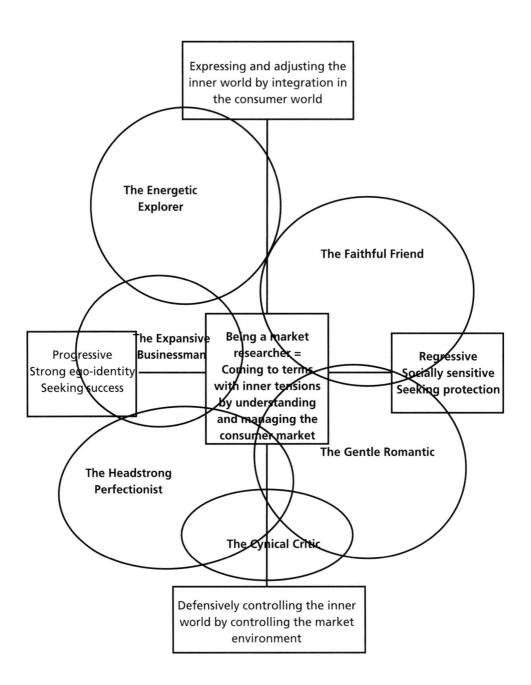

Expressing and adjusting the inner world by integration in the consumer world

The Energetic Explorer

The Faithful Friend

The Expansive Businessman

Progressive
Strong ego-identity
Seeking success

Being a market researcher =
Coming to terms with inner tensions by understanding and managing the consumer market

Regressive
Socially sensitive
Seeking protection

The Gentle Romantic

The Headstrong Perfectionist

The Cynical Critic

Defensively controlling the inner world by controlling the market environment

Hints to help colleagues and clients choose the suitable market researcher

As I said, this description of what market research could in fact be, and the — caricatured — typology of my colleagues market researchers, is a conceptual exercise. To be honest, it was an expedition full of surprises, but also hard excavation work with numerous corrections to locate the right spots. Sometimes I have been dreaming and fantasizing, at other times I felt firmly with my two feet on the ground. Sometimes a touch of cynicism has crept in. In the end, writing this document gave me great satisfaction. It was a way of releasing my restlessness, and made me feel more in control and more harmonious. Yet, I am not fully satisfied. I have a feeling that I have not grasped the totality, a feeling that some pieces of the puzzle do not yet fit. Guess what type of complex and ambivalent type of market researcher is writing this!

If this exercise had been worked out more thoroughly in a really profound study we could have drawn a number of interesting conclusions which would have been meaningful not only for marketing people but also for my fellow workers. As I said, it could have given our clients an idea of how to choose the type of market researcher with who they best embark upon a certain type of research or product. It could have helped my employer or my colleagues to make the right choice when staffing certain functions...

The 'Energetic Explorer' is perhaps more interesting when we are dealing with an international study or when a full measure of innovation and great daring is needed... For very global or creative studies, the 'Faithful Friends' could be the right choice. They are also excellent team leaders, certainly, unless one wants to widen one's activities. If this is the case, we would probably recommend the expansive type, although this type also disposes of more talents as a sales manager... If you want a dutiful and obedient researcher, you should rather think of the 'Gentle Romantic', if at least you remain aware of his dreamy weaknesses... Does the client want to see profound and detailed analytic results? Then the 'Headstrong Perfectionist' would be the right choice — as long as no strict deadline is set... Does Censydiam need a new director or do we wish to expand? Then we have to call in the 'Expansive Businessman'... And... But why not fill out the rest yourself?

After she graduated as a sociologist, **Madeleine Janssens** *took the postgraduate course of specialized licentiate in Marketing, at the Gent University.*

Madeleine has been with Censydiam from the very beginning. Since 1986, when she joined us, she has been active in the field of qualitative diagnostic research, two years of which she spent in the Netherlands. Since 1991, she has been managing the Qualitative Research Division in Belgium. She also coordinates joint ventures all over the world and especially in the Middle East.

At the end of this millennium, Madeleine ponders whether the next will be that of the women. Madeleine, a feminist? Hardly. "Why did men feel the need for male dominance?" she asks us. "Did women also not profit from it sometimes? If not, why would women – who, intrinsically are as strong as men, be it in other areas – have let it happen?"

Madeleine gives us here an insight into the singularity of humankind in general, and men and women in particular.

The sex of the world in the third millennium

Are the sexes out of balance?

"Women conquer the business world" — "Sex change for managers?" — "Career women cause more stress among men" — Headlines in the press. 'Girl Power', 'Emotional Intelligence' — Vogue words or signs of the times?

What kind of beings are they, those men and women? Have women been created from the floating rib of men, as the story of the Creation makes us believe? Are women man's best friends, as my brothers liked to say when teasing their sisters? Are men, in essence, helpless beings who would never have been what they are without the support of women? Do we find a strong woman behind every strong man whereas a strong woman can fight her own battles? Is she less interesting in the matrimonial market?

At the end of this second millennium, the relationships between the sexes are changing. Today, new criteria define the meaning of being a man or a woman. Tomorrow, society will put different values concerning social functioning first; other values that appraise the feminization of society positively and even encourage it. Will tomorrow's managers be 'feminine' considering that the qualities of the feminine way of being answer better to the requirements of future management? Or will dominance and authoritarian demeanor, which according to the classical feminists are typically masculine, induce men — out of sheer protection of his power and position — to check this evolution?

Tensions — due to attraction and rejection — have always characterized the relations between the sexes, not only through the ages but also across different cultures. Anthropologist Margaret Mead (1901–1978) thought it worth the effort to devote a study to the phenomenon. "Male and Female" (1949) has become a standard work of anthropological and sociological studies. History also shows that man has always tried to exercise power — 'brute' power, according to feminists — over women. In the second century BC, the Roman statesman Cato the Elder called on his fellow citizens to maintain all laws by which former generations had curtailed women's power and say. He warned: "As soon as women become man's equals, they take the upper hand."

Why did men feel the need for male dominance? Was it blind and absolute dominance or did women also profit from it sometimes? If not, why would women – who, if we may believe Cato's words, intrinsically are as strong as men, be it in other areas – have let it happen?

An insight into the singularity of humankind in general, and men and women in particular, could put us on our way.

How Censydiam portrays man: a view of the human kind

Women, just like men, are individuals with a complex configuration of ever-changing interactions between need and fulfillment. Both are individuals with time-depending motives to reach a certain state of satisfaction. If we wish to understand both, it is important to get a basic insight into their needs and satisfactions. An exploration into the behavior and motivations of humankind may seem to be a difficult journey. In order to stay on course, Censydiam offers a specific view of men and women by which men and women are seen as 'global human beings' composed of emotions, fears, and desires. In this way, we obtain a psychodynamic view of people, a view that enables us to acquire an understanding of both rational and subconscious decisions that drive even the simplest behavior. The framework that holds this model together has been described in detail in 'The Naked Consumer' and in 'Motivational Research Revisited'. Here we will concentrate on those elements of the model that are helpful to illustrate our argument.

Our portrayal of man assumes that every individual – man and woman – is born into a divided world in which the source of needs – the *nature* of the individual – is separated from the source of satisfaction – the environment or *culture*, the *social context* in which the individual lives. In order to survive, men and women try to bridge the gap between the two worlds. Through a process of trial and error, they develop a personal 'blueprint,' a record of the methods they have learned for achieving satisfaction within a given social environment. This blueprint serves as a frame of reference when making – subconscious – decisions.

In the presence of a cultural environment holding a number of possibilities that are different for men and women, the individual tries to resolve feelings of tension, inferiority, and dissatisfaction. Not only the cultural environment offers the different sexes different possibilities; their nature also – their genetic potential, their inner nature – is different. Which came first, the chicken or the egg? The social environment – culture – which influenced the inner nature and modeled it or the inner nature which recognized the strong and the weak points of both sexes and determined different roles for each, so that they could make the best use of their potential? Although everyone will agree that men and women are different, it is unclear for the majority of us in what sense they differ. Still, if we want to understand the relations between the sexes and describe the changes in these relations, it is important to arrive at such an understanding of these differences so that it strengthens the feeling of self-esteem and at the same time the mutual trust, the individual feeling of responsibility, and the cooperation.

By means of a unique process Censydiam charts these expressions, demonstrations and motivations which indicate the path a person chooses to take in any given circumstance. Therefore, we draw a map.

A vertical axis outlines an individual dimension. It indicates how people – men and women – express their innate, intrinsic potential, their inner nature. At the top of this axis, contact with the outside world is seen as a source of inspiration and submission. At the bottom, fear is so intense that an area is defined and margins are established within which experiences are allowed to be undergone.

The horizontal axis deals with the way in which the social environment offers possibilities to express one's individual views – one's culture. Here the environment is a source of advancement, which is primarily impressed upon men. On the other hand, the environment may be a source of security, which through the times has been impressed on women.

We can represent this visually by the following diagram.

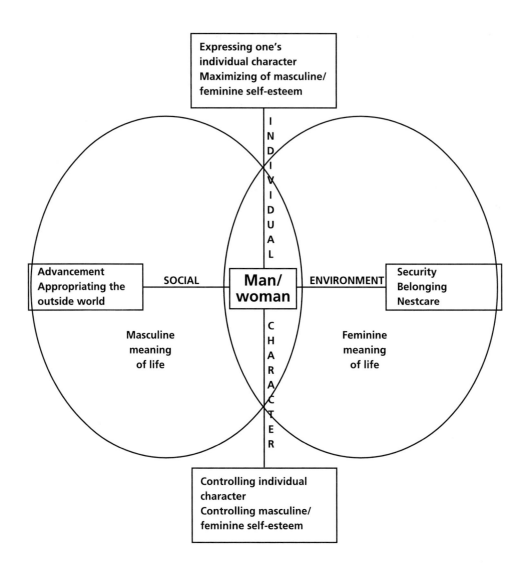

Nature and culture:
different starting positions for men and women

As we said before, every one of us – man or woman – is born into a divided world in which the source of needs – the individual and his inner nature – is separated from the source of satisfaction – the environment or culture in which he is brought into the world. Therefore, it is important to amplify on the basic difference between nature and culture and its effect on the masculine and feminine meaning of life.

The *inner nature* of an individual comprises al his inherent potentialities, his wishes and desires, his urges and his instincts. In essence it is that which is born and is still 'pure' and unaffected by outside influences. In this sense, the nature of an individual is egocentric and follows its own motives. In order to make it possible for individuals to coexist, a certain harmony of the individual motives in accordance with a collective aim – in which the individual also has a certain interest – is no luxury. After all, 'living together' is not possible when everyone works towards his individual goal. It is strictly impossible in a society that is confronted with a tough society – such as our forebears lived in before the industrial revolution – in which one needs to 'work together' in order to survive as a species and one has to appeal on the strongest qualities of each of the individual participants.

The consequence is that it is 'necessary' to channel, to regulate or 'cultivate' individual desires and needs so that they will not go their own way. The intensity of this regulation essentially depends on the intensity with which it is necessary to unite forces to progress as a society and so it is partly determined by the aim to prosper. It is characteristic however for such a regulation within human forms of coexistence that human society is often reticent about changing regulations. Every modification indeed implies a transitional phase in which the solidity of the prevailing norms are being questioned and whether or not it will gradually – through evolution – or abruptly – through revolution – make way for differently colored norms. These changes may therefore imply a disruption of a stable social order in that it makes it easy for natural urges, wishes, and desires to 'escape' social control. A society must be able and willing to deal constructively with such a disruption.

From what precedes it is clear that *culture* — in the primary sense of the word — has to do with regulating the nature of individual members of a particular society and, by extension, with the different categories of individuals, namely men and women. The cultural singularity of a society is the result of the way in which the urges, wishes, and desires of the individuals are being modulated. Culture is a filter, a prism that determines how the inner nature of an individual will be expressed.

When we look further at the different cultures, we also come to the conclusion that a society that has to deal with harsh conditions of life and thus experiences a — physical — threat to survival tends to protect its biological potential for the future. Women are at the center of this biological potential. Women will be especially safeguarded and protected. Consequently, the strong point of the women was the care for the family and this would be strengthened. Feminine 'values' such as caring for others, belonging, support of the men, comfort and so forth became 'added values' that increased the chances of survival for the group in the future. In most cultures this has been translated into directing women towards domestic life and screening them off from social life in the outside world — the 'housewife'. Over the years, this screening off from social life has become part of a social way of living and hence a sociological fact.

This 'guarding' of biological potential underlies the division of the sexes within cultures. It is consistent with the fact that in most cultures overmastering and protecting the living habitat lies within the domain of the men. In his book 'Man as Myth,' David Gilmore relates manhood cults with the harshness and the self-discipline required for the manly role. Because of their stronger muscular strength, men were better equipped physically to assume this role. In addition, their lesser value in the field of biological potential allowed them to run more risks: one man could produce as many children as there were women available; one woman could only bear one child a year regardless of the number of men available. Men had to assume a more extraverted role. Manly 'values' such as power, capability, expansion, dominance, authority and so on became 'added values' that increased the chances of survival of the group. Men who performed best according to these values had in fact the best chances of survival and hence the best chances to procreate these qualities in the following generations. With that knowledge at the back of our minds we can put that the feminists do the men wrong when they reproach them with having these qualities. Genetic selection of men based on these qualities guaranteed the survival of men as appropriately as genetic selection of women based on care for the family did for women. Women too benefited from it.

Yet, this benefit no longer remains a benefit as society begins to enjoy more prosperity. The more a society enjoys prosperity the less associating masculine and feminine meanings of life with 'gender' as such becomes a necessity. Both roles — the extrovert role of dominance of the environment against the introvert care for the family — remain necessary but need not be realized in such a sharply gender-divided way. There is more room for overflow among men and women.

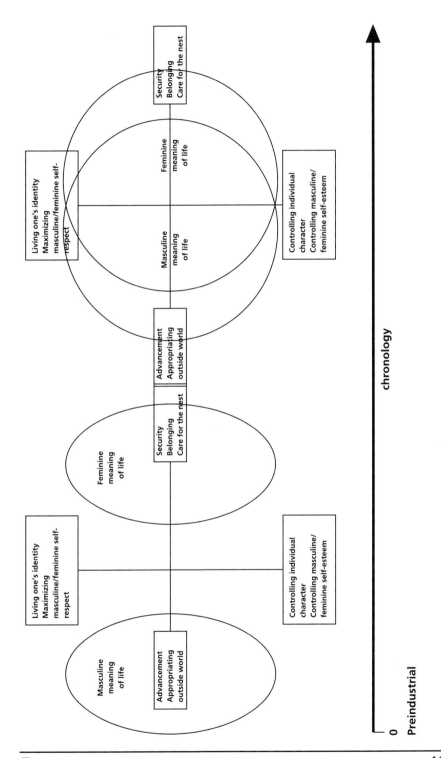

Men especially seem to have a problem with the overflow from the feminine way of being to the masculine meaning of life. This made Antonia and Theo Schoenaker say: "The development of women is necessary indeed, but men do not easily swallow this, just like the development of democracy sticks in the throats of potentates and provokes fear of the new, unfamiliar situation. Fear of a possible superiority of hitherto suppressed persons or groupings may also be an issue here." And further: "Those who block the progress to equality head for a crisis, not only in marriage or in the family but also in education, in politics and in society itself." In his 'Liefde in tijden van eenzaamheid' ['Love in Times of Solitude'], Paul Verhaeghe reasons from similar premises: "The three peoples of the Book — Jews, Christians and Muslims — each in their own way have put women as well as eroticism in a bad spot. The fact that, little by little, women as well as eroticism are able to escape from it is not without consequences. The first and foremost consequences are confusion and distrust with men, aggression, and flight. And an attempt to go back to former times."

Time now to make an excursion into other cultures.

Women in different cultures

Do women in other cultures look differently at being a woman? Are these differences to be traced to the nature of women or are they steered from culture, which adjusts the expressions of womanly nature?

Many years of experience with international research has given Censydiam the possibility to get to know women in different cultures and try to understand what really moves them in their womanhood. We shall look at three very unlike cultures, the Arab, the Chinese, and the Western.

Different research objectives in different cultures, in which we explored the specific meaning of femininity with women themselves, have shown that the basic characteristics of the womanly nature appear to be sensibility, sentiment, and a receptive/responsive attitude with respect to the surrounding world. This is in contrast with the down-to-earthly, rational, strong, no-nonsense ego-expansive nature of their male counterparts. Besides, being a woman rests on two important pillars: femininity and motherhood. In each case, both aspects show totally different sides of feminine being although they are linked. Femininity is described as those elements that express the elegance, the refinement, and the culture of the women – elements that put women into relief in their – physical – beauty. It is an 'instrument' of seduction – and following that, the realization of the biological potential. Motherhood is linked directly with care of the family. It includes everything connected with tenderness, softness, and warmth. It is defined by a caring attitude towards others, in the first place the children but also the husband and housekeeping in general.

When we ask women in *Chinese society* what 'being a woman' means to them, we find that – at first – the main emphasis is laid on women's economical independence. This independence, combined with the fact that women also perform most of the household activities, gives Chinese women a feeling of power and pride. Indeed, they often suggest that they are not just the equals of their husbands but that they might very well be better and stronger. They are not only good at their tasks, in their function of mothers and wives they are also very important to society. Most Chinese women seem to feel respected by society as far as their socioeconomic position is concerned. During Mao Zedong's times, it was indeed pointed out than men and women 'were equals,' than men and women should contribute equally to make society progress. In fact, for women it came down to suppressing their feminine nature; there was no room for 'bourgeois, feminine behavior' and women should act according to the rules and norms of the masculine nature. Jung Chan's 'Wild Swans, Three Daughters of China,' paints a striking portrait of how femininity and feminine nature were positively valued during the Manchu Dynasty – although the object of femininity was to present women as ornamental objects for men and not to bring forth their self-respect – but were maligned during Mao. Also how women had to conform with masculine values and norms but remained, in everyday life and within the party, 'inferior' to men.

This has surely been strongly influenced by the self-preservation of the masculine nature but also by the fact that men and women cannot be put on the same level by decree. One cannot pass over the evolution of masculine and feminine meanings of life. Feminine nature cannot be written off by a 'Little Red Book,' even if contains quotations from Chairman Mao himself. That does not alter the fact that Mao Zedong's influence is still felt today in the ways women talk about their womanhood. They have almost lost the ability of coming into contact with their deepest feminine being. They are embarrassed of talking about the subject. Extra securing and a very cautious approach were needed to make the theme debatable. The central issue however is that the seeds of the feminine meaning of life are still present, deeply hidden sometimes, sometimes coming to the surface.

What are the primary values of this womanly way of being? We noticed that Chinese women attributed 'femininity' to married women only and even more so to mothers. In this, we are in fact close here to the care for the family. The majority of Chinese women are even convinced that young girls do not have a clue as to what being a woman is really about. They have a feeling that young girls do not behave very differently from young boys. Only after marriage do girls develop into 'fully feminine' women and, finally, motherhood brings them the experience needed to develop femininity altogether.

Within marriage itself the perception of femininity if often one of self-sacrifice. The most 'feminine' women are generally seen as women who are dedicated to love and care for their husband and child. Who would have thought so after the solemn proclamation of the – economic – independence of women?

Next to motherhood in the physical sense – i.e. being able to have a child – and in the emotional sense – being able to love and care, to support others – respondents bring up another fundamental element of femininity, namely womanhood. However, in this respect, Chinese women do not want to put too much emphasis on the external qualities of attractiveness, sensuality, and seductiveness. One should never overdo the external 'adornments.' What counts is the inner being of a woman, her virtue. They declare that virtue and morality are the cornerstones of their upbringing and matters of great importance in distinguishing between women 'with a good heart' and women 'with a bad heart.' They often believe that women have and should have stricter morals than men, to make sure that the family and in fact society as a whole function in a peaceful way.

As for *Arab society*, it appears that Arab women perceive the difference between the masculine and feminine ways of being as a notable characteristic of their society – especially with regard to the perception that the Western world has of the relations between the sexes. This is understandable when one sees that Arab culture defines the norm of being a woman in a very basic manner. The main points are clearly and almost explicitly the values of sensibility, sentiment, and a receptive/responsive attitude towards the surrounding world.

Compared to the motivations of Western society, these basic motivations are more strictly connected with gender as an objective fact from which one cannot deviate on the basis of personality. This involves that the distinction and the expectations as to gender role are clearly outlined and that there are fewer overflows between the masculine and feminine ways of being. It also involves that there is a sharply defined frame of reference, according to which men and women should concretely behave. Some women perceive

MADELEINE JANSSENS

these strictly defined expectations as a compass by which they can go in their contacts with the outside world. Others experience it as a constraint and think that they should exteriorize their feminine being within the bounds of the prescribed cultural values.

In practice, the division of roles between men and women give cause to a complex tangle of 'submission' and 'playing an enterprising part in the outside world from behind the scenes.' Women see men almost as the equivalent of social rules and norms. In this sense, they affirm that men tend to subject women as much as possible, that men are forced to do so to maintain their position but also that the continuation of the present order in society depends on it. Yet, women are sufficiently 'intuitive and clever' to allow men their credit when it comes to exerting their influence in the outside world but will also use their cunning to exert their own influence in a subdued manner, such as through their sons.

In *Western society*, women recognize that – in relation to men – women are characterized by a higher degree of sensibility, tenderness, emotion, human involvement, and a greater degree of social concern and care for their environment. This sensible, caring character of women is directly related to thier biological individuality, that is to say their fecundity, to the potential mother every women knows she is. Even if the woman has or gets no children, she is commonly identified by the characteristics that stem from her caring motherly instinct.

Women perceive the caring role of the 'mother figure' as the traditional task of women. On the one hand she is caring, owing to her biological instinct to care for the nest – just like the animals – and on the other hand traditional society expects her to do so. She has always done it, from a sense of duty – bearing children, caring for them, caring for her husband, for the home. However, women emphasize that in the course of time the traditional pattern has undergone some changes. They refer to the greater equality between men and women, which enables women to make a career, to be as independent as men are, and to have time for themselves. Yet, one feels that this has more to do with forms of expression – the packaging – than with their intrinsic way of being. Nothing essential has changed. This brings with it that some women point out that they may have experienced a change of norms but that this is not compensated by a change of norms for men. After all, men are at the receiving end. Therefore, men have a feeling that women with children who have a job have entered into a double contract, that of caring for the family and another of advancement, of conquering the outside world. This burdens their lives and may occasion conflicts between their caring, motherly feelings as a homemaker and their ambitions to broaden their horizons, which necessitates experiences in the outside world.

These observations show us that the feminine way of being gets its meaning and content from values that are quite uniform. Culture however gives the direction in which these fundamental values will be expressed and to what extent culture defines the role of the sexes either in a strictly gender-linked way — such as in traditional Arab culture — or leaving room for expressing one's personal potential — such as in Western culture. This interpretation got the discussion going with my female Arab colleagues at Censydiam. They told me that I, as a Western woman, enjoyed more freedom, that women in Western culture could go out to work, dispose of their own money, could realize themselves... They did not immediately understand that many women in the West consider going out to work a duty and a necessity to make ends meet — and not a freedom or a form of self-realization — and that the money they earn is not pocket money but extra housekeeping money.

The feminization of society

We have seen that, as a society begins to develop more wealth, linking masculine and feminine ways of being strictly with gender as such becomes less of a necessity. A society that has no longer to deal with harsh conditions that threaten survival can accept that different rules and norms guide social life and even appreciate these positively. As society is again threatened in its fundamental being – in times of war for example – we see people revert to the basic values which prescribe men to fight the danger and protect women and children – the biological potential.

In our Western society, fortunately, the stage of survival lies beyond us. People in our society can turn their thoughts to 'living' rather than 'surviving.' Because of this, one cannot only see a shift in values on the social level but also in the balance between the sexes.

Let us first look at the *social level.* 'Survival cultures,' which set great store by the physical protection of the outside world, – and men by their physical strength were best suited to do that, – attached great importance to these values. Values such as (physical) strength, capability, dominance, authority, and so on, combined with clever and reasoned insight – 'political capability' so to say – became added values which roused social prestige and success – muscles and brains. Those values were appreciated by men as well as by women and justified control of women by men. As society developed, actual physical protection of the outside world became less necessary. Society however still found great benefit in the physical superiority of men. Agrarian as well as industrial activity needed physically strong men who also had a good share of intelligence. Women could have insight but lacked the necessary physical capability to apply it and so a 'reason' continued to exist to keep her in an inferior position. Moreover, one should not forget that men – once they have had a taste of power and raised it to an 'acquired status' – will not willingly let women endanger their territory even if they would be capable of doing so. The masculine ideologies force men to play their roles on pain of losing their identity, a threat that proves to be worse that death. (David Gilmore) Owing to the fact that men generally have political or judicial power and that they are bigger and stronger, they can compel women to be obliging, if conventional morality has not already done so. This made Emma Goldman come to the conclusion, in 1910, that "in the first place, marriage is an economic agreement, an insurance policy. The only difference with an ordinary life insurance is that it demands more and binds you more. If, however, woman's premium is a husband, she pays for it with her name, her privacy, her self-respect, her very life, 'until death doth part.' Besides, the marriage insurance condemns her to lifelong dependence, to parasitism, to utter uselessness, in a personal as well as in a social way." (Emma Goldman (1869–1940), Anarchism and Other Essays, "*Marriage and Love*", 1910).

Our present society does no longer need physically overpowering men. As society evolves to a tertiary stadium, the main points are insight, intelligence, intuition, sensibility, and acting and reacting on the basis of this input. Physical qualities no longer give one status and prestige, but these 'spiritualized' values do. Besides, these values are also part of the feminine way of being: they are not the exclusive domains of men.

This changing sociocultural slant brings with it that feminine ways of being are getting more room for expression. However, it also entails that masculine control of women can no longer be justified or, what is more, it can no longer stand in the way of feminine contribution to society. David Barash (*The Hare and the Tortoise*) feels that feminism – and the feminization of society – is not unique to recent decades. According to David Barash, forerunners of feminism can be found in almost every phase of human history. What is unique is its intensity, its dissemination and the greater expandability in Western culture today. It clearly is a cultural phenomenon that is strikingly present in some societies and absent in others. According to Barash, it surely not genetically determined: it is connected with a complex of social and cultural values.

It is in the context of this social evolution that we can place the emergence of the Girl Power movement and phenomena such as 'emotional intelligence.'

The *Girl Power* movement is the result of a growing awareness of young women that they have a social self-esteem – an added value, when compared with the former generation – which they want to discover and experience to the full. "I am I, and I can stand up for my rights" is their creed. It has nothing to do with the Women's Lib of the sixties and the seventies although they both originate with the affirmation of women. Whereas Women's Lib aimed at equal treatment of the sexes and tried to realize it on the basis of the masculine values which at that time were the standard and the guarantee of social added value, the Girl Power movement makes more self-willed and more self-conscious choices. It does not imply a disavowal of the feminine way of being; it centers, at most, extreme focus on those feminine values that can be appreciated in our society of today. It brings with it the risk that they lose sight of the overall view of being a woman – the caring aspects which are, for example, interwoven with motherly values. From settled quarters this sometimes causes reproaches such as egocentrism, freedom gone astray, and a lack of responsibility; things one can get away with when one is a capable – single – girl in her twenties but one will have to be abandon when taking up family responsibility in order to get more balance and stability. Women's Liberation comments that all this has been made possible only because Women's Lib paved the way and that Girl Power just only wants reap the sweet fruits instead of proposing a constructive and relevant headway.

All this has its consequences on the way in which they look at the other sex. Young women do not want to be considered less important than anyone else is. Even if they are, in practice, they do want to get rid of the feeling. Men however are being put on the defensive and even pushed into submission. Girl Power says: we are all beautiful girls and we know that we are worthy of being desired and loved by boys; and since we are what the boys want, we are in charge. "Male contest, female choice" is still very much alive today. Within this line of reasoning, the boy becomes a sexual object.

It is clear that these days Girl Power is a much-differentiated movement with widely divergent trends and visions. It surely is the consequence of the stage in which the movement finds itself today. Now that the time is ripe for it, things have to be sorted out, unorthodox choices have to be made, and the movement should avoid falling into the trap of ideological patterns. Whether it will be ready to leave the playground stage and march on to a social movement that will have a structural influence on tomorrow's society is still the question. If not, it will surely have its impact on the next trend.

Emotional intelligence. The former definition of intelligence — pure reason if you want — chiefly stresses intellectual, purposive qualities. It is a definition that situates intelligence in the left half of the brain. This definition has a positive appreciation of logical and rational thinking that is able to analyze and draw strategic conclusions. These are the qualities of the intelligence that have surely served men very well as rulers and protectors of the outside world in harsh forms of society and that continued to gain in importance through natural selection. Those who had more of all this had more chances to pass on these qualities to their descendants. The question is whether all this is still important today and cannot usefully be completed. The need is no longer for survival but for making life more pleasant. Intelligence has to make room for qualities that give more color and more soul to life.

Emotional intelligence is an approach of intelligence that also puts the stress on the right hemisphere of the brain, the part of intuition, empathy, and emotion. It is the heart, the warm character of intelligence. The old definition appeared no longer adapted to the necessities of the new social reality in which feminine values got more and more room to express themselves and in which their relative significance and complement to the down-to-earth qualities of the rational intelligence became clear. Emotional intelligence however does not claim the dominance of the functions of the right hemisphere; it rather stresses the synergy between the functions of the left and right parts of the brain.

Of course, this social evolution also has its influence on the *relations between the sexes.* Since we have to deal here with men and women, we should look at them separately.

As far as men are concerned, we find that they are confronted with a diminished feeling of importance. Their feeling of added value is on the wane. They sense that they are no longer self-evidently empowered on the social level. They are increasingly often confronted with the typically gender-connected qualities of women which also gain their social relevance. Women can no longer be disposed of as weak and incompetent; quite contrary they appear to become stronger and more resolute, not physically but mentally. Women have their self-esteem; they do no longer need men.

Cato seems to be proved right when he declares that women get the upper hand as soon as they are put in an equal position with men. The crucial question is how men react to this. Can they put something in its place that restores their self-esteem? (Hypothesis #1) Or will they more likely – out of a primal reflex – tend to go on the defensive? (Hypothesis #2) Or will he stoically accept everything and submit to the new situation? (Hypothesis #3)

We can detect few signals that substantiate the first hypothesis. This is no surprise as we see that in the course of time men always have learned to fend for themselves, either in an offensive way (hypothesis #2) or in the defensive way of fleeing if they cannot win (hypothesis #2). In her book *De gesjeesde man* [Man as a dropout], Natalie Gittelson assumes that it is the dream of feminism that men and women would find each other in a new, happy relationship as soon as male dominance had disappeared. However, it does not seem to go that way. Men feel that they are confronted with contradictory reproaches – that they are the dominators and suppressors on the one hand and, on the other hand, no longer adequate. Therefore, many drop out, many grow farther away from women instead of going part of the way to meet them. Gittelson also maintains that it increasingly happens that more accommodating men, who have done their best to adapt to the changing situation, see their marriage go on the rocks, while marriages of the traditional type, with an authoritarian man who could not care less about emancipation, remain unaffected by the feminine evolution of society.

Men also seem to be guided by the concern about what they could loose and much less by new opportunities. World history has demonstrated repeatedly that this fear leads to the rigid positions of an autocratic leader. The effect of it is that men begin to move slowly, that they are not accommodating, and try with all their strength to block the developments that have already outstripped them. Only 'emotionally intelligent' men succeed in dealing with this in a constructive way.

Now the *feminine side*. Those who think that all women undividedly applaud this evolution will be disappointed. It was the case for me when we did research into the perception of being a woman in Arab society. It was an eye-opening experience to see that not all women shared the Western ethnocentric vision which tells us that the suppression of Arab women is a 'plight.' Some – specifically those who give content to their femininity out of an adaptive strategy – feel fine about it. They get security and comfort from 'male dominance.' Would it not be arrogant to tell that they find themselves in a bad plight? What would be a bad plight for them is to see this balance between men and women disturbed. They do not see disturbing the traditional pattern broaden their possibilities or create new opportunities. It only inspires fear and uncertainty. However, we need not travel all the way to the Arab world to hear this. Women among my acquaintances, too, do not always acclaim this development. My youngest sister finds the highest satisfaction in her caring role of a mother. Yet, she has been exposed to the same standard of values as her sisters and is the child of a mother who saw the self-realization of her daughters in the same way as that of her sons. My sister thinks that she has 'a much better life' than I and other of her older sisters who are always 'on the move' as she puts it. As long as all of us find satisfaction in the things we are personally engaged with and how we give meaning to our lives, there is no reason to try to convince the others of the opposite.

How does it come then that many women do not look forward to their peers' growing social weight with greater pleasure? Barash explains this from the difference between nature and culture. This explanation can give us additional insight into the masculine reticence with respect to this evolution. Their evolutionary past has strengthened women's feminine values of support, obedience, submission, care for the family, and placing oneself in the service of others. This was their nature, their genetic predestination as it were, just as it was for men to dominate and to protect the biological potential for the future. It is not because in a few decades the social environment shifts the helm that nature makes the same turn around with ease. In his book *The Hare and the Tortoise*, David Barash presents us with the image of a circus artist who runs a race with his left foot on a hare and his right on a tortoise. The tortoise represents the slowly progressing biological evolution and the hare our cultural evolution, which will always run faster – especially now and even more so in the future. It is understood that this shaky balance will also assert its influence on the relations between the sexes.

The third millennium
On our way to a new men/women relations.

From the above we can put the question of what biological evolution has in store for our ambivalent creature. Shall we shape our culture or otherwise? It is unthinkable that, in some respects, we would be less biologically determined and it is also improbable that culture would exert less influence than it does now. Yet, we will remain subjected to natural selection. As long as certain people will have more progeny than others – for whatever reason – selection will take place and the pool of genes of the population will shift in their direction.

Yet, this selection will not only – as usual – be to slow to come into balance with cultural evolution, let alone counter it. It will also become less and less 'natural.' As people are getting more information about birth control, rational considerations will determine future parents' reproductive success. Besides that, the 'fertility economy' makes 'parents' redundant. So it happened some months ago that my sister, who as a physician specializes in 'making women pregnant,' was confronted with the nineteen-year-old granny of one of her patients who had been fertilized in vitro. "Oh, doctor, isn't that marvelous! Now we don't even need a man for it anymore!" was her reaction when she was told about in vitro fertilization.

Well, men will still be needed, if only to produce the seed. The choice however is ever more the women's, surely when they ever free themselves more from male 'dominance.' Still, just because of it, they are confronted with a paradox. Natural selection occurs only as far as certain individuals have more descendants than others or when certain genes make more copies of themselves than others do. Because of his biological nature, one individual man is capable of a much greater reproduction than an individual woman is. And it is unlikely that women as a group will give preference to one type of man with a particular genetic heritage only in order to steer natural selection in one or another direction.

Relations between the sexes will certainly not become easier in the future. As the lives of men and women run along certain predisposed tendencies, men and women will have to develop a clear picture of what they want for themselves and for the world in which they live. They will have to make choices. Making choices is very tempting as long as one is denied them. It becomes more awkward when one is forced to do something and it is no longer a choice of not doing it. Besides, the relations between the sexes should not get the character of a theater of war such as the feminists of the beginning – and even today – defined it. The social evolution allows for an exchange between masculine and feminine ways of being. It brings about that men can show their feminine traits – which they also possess – without being called effeminate and that women also can give free rein to their masculine features without embarrassing their male partner – "she wears the pants." This means that men and women can externalize themselves more through their qualities of 'human beings' whereas until now they had to act in respect to their gender.

It would however be regrettable that the overflow between masculine and feminine ways of being would be of such a nature that the similarities became stronger than the differences. Differences should remain. Not only do they lend color but they also provide some healthy, inspiring tensions and attractions. Besides, many women adore sitting together with friends for a good kaffeeklatsch with 'complaints' about their husbands. It is not that there is much to complain but it is the wives' way to recapitulate that without them men just only make a mess of it. Would it not be a pity then that men, at the end of the third millenium, would only be found at 'sperm farms' as one women we met in a group interview let slip in a futurological moment? We are confident that 'intelligent' women will not let this happen.